Erica Sosna

YOUR

LIFE

PLAN

How to set yourself on the right path
and take charge of your life

CAPSTONE

Registered office

John Wiley and Sons Ltd, The Atrium, Southern Gate, Chichester, West Sussex, PO19 8SQ, United Kingdom

For details of our global editorial offices, for customer services and for information about how to apply for permission to reuse the copyright material in this book please see our website at www.wiley.com.

Library of Congress Cataloging-in-Publication Data

Sosna, Erica.
    Your life plan : how to set yourself on the right path and take charge of your life / Erica Sosna.
        pages cm
    Includes bibliographical references and index.
    ISBN 978-0-85708-486-6 (pbk. : alk. paper)   1. Success–Psychological aspects.   2. Self-actualization (Psychology)   3. Change (Psychology)   I. Title.
    BF637.S8S646 2014
    158–dc23
                              2013048408

A catalogue record for this book is available from the British Library.

ISBN 978-0-857-08486-6 (pbk) ISBN 978-0-857-08489-7 (ebk)
ISBN 978-0-857-08487-3 (ebk)

Cover design by Mackerel Ltd
Original illustrations by Curtis Allen (www.curtisallen.co.uk)
Set in 10 on 13 pt SabonLTStd by Toppan Best-set Premedia Limited
Printed in Great Britain by TJ International Ltd, Padstow, Cornwall, UK

For my grandmother, Rima Sosna, whose love,
wisdom and experience has taught me courage.

CONTENTS

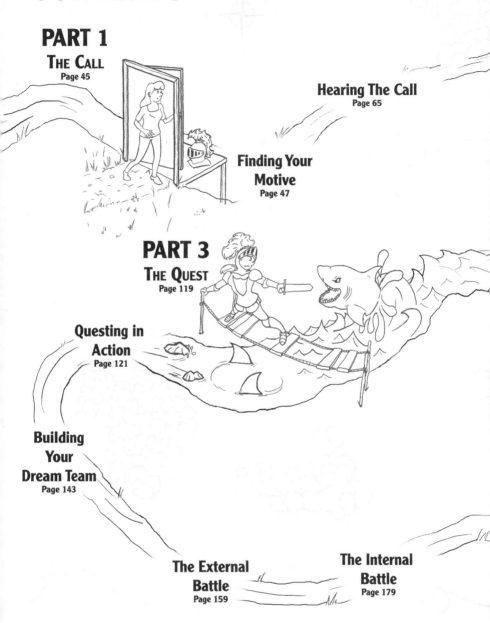

INTRODUCTION

II The art of navigation is to know where
you are, where you are going and how to
get there safely. *II*
Sailors Almanac

Welcome to *Your Life Plan*. A practical book to help you navigate your life and be the hero in your own story.

How are you feeling today, right now? Disgruntled, tired, curious, excited, neutral? What created that feeling? How are you feeling about your life in general? About your existence, your contribution, your success, your relationships?

Stop a moment. Listen to your environment. See it in action around you.

How much of your life feels like your choice? How close is your reality to the life you would like to live?

This book is a practical course in how to choose and then live a life that is meaningful, exciting and adventurous for you. Everyone's life project is unique. Having a life project – a dream or goal that feels like a real challenge, can give you focus, energy and purpose.

If you set yourself a Quest to start today, right now, what would it be? If you are already on a journey toward a goal, what would be most helpful in getting you to your destination?

These are the questions this book can help with.

My aim is to help you be the hero or heroine in your own life.

When I say hero, I don't necessarily mean the cape, the tights and the clenched fist. Only one of my heroes, Freddie Mercury, came with the full regalia. When we think about heroes or heroines, we think about people who took action on what they believed in, were courageous, determined, creative; people who changed themselves, their world or the environment in some lasting way. All of us possess the capability to do this in the right context and given the right support. If you are going to stretch for your dreams, you are going to need to awaken the hero (or heroine) within.

Being heroic doesn't mean you will always have a happy ending. I can't guarantee that if you use the tools in this book, everything will work out exactly the way you would like it to. What I can promise, is that the experience of setting out on a journey and taking steps to realize a dream or ambition, will bring you all kinds of benefits, adventures and value that you would not experience if you stayed where you are.

As a society, we love the idea of the hero. How many songs, from the sublime to the ridiculous, include this word? How many refer to it indirectly, the experience of doing something remarkable or unusual, perhaps once in a lifetime or as a way of living? So much of our film, fiction and theatre is all built around a central character who we root for and watch evolve over a period of time. And we humans love to share real life stories that speak powerfully about what we can achieve when we put our minds to it.

Over the last ten years, I have worked with hundreds of people of all ages, using the structure of stories, the idea of the hero, and the skills of project management to help them to find their inner hero and create what they want for themselves. I've helped people downsize, change careers, find a relationship, rebuild a relationship with a loved one, relocate across the globe, pass their exams, overcome anxiety disorders, set up a business, and find balance in their work lives.

There is nothing in the world that I am more passionate about, or good at, than helping people clarify and catalyze their own direction. That's my purpose in life . . .

. . . to help you find yours.

So, you are in good hands.

As a coach and consultant, I've found that seeing a client's life as a story can be a very effective tool for working on their life path and choices. When you begin to see yourself as a character and your life as a plot, you notice the patterns and the "plot line" in the journey you have taken so far. You begin to empathize with yourself as the hero, on an uncertain path, doing the best you can, and the themes and dreams that surround you take on a mythical quality. This sense of being part of a larger narrative, integral to the world around you, playing a part in the stories of others, connects us both with our ancestors and with the present.

Our story can help us to make choices about the changes we want to make or the adventures we want to go on. I've always loved a good story and I've noticed that whatever age we are, we become as rapt as children when someone offers to tell us a tale. When I trained as a storyteller for grown-ups, I noticed that stories could be educational, inspiring and even life saving. They often reflect universal truths about humanity and how life happens.

In every great story the world over, whether fiction or historical, there are heroes and heroines. Flawed, passionate human beings who take themselves on an adventure beyond the ordinary and every day. They overcome challenges, find love, learn new things and return transformed by their experiences. In this book, I will help you uncover your heroic nature, decide on a Quest and design and implement your own Life Plan. We will work together to find and manifest your very own Heroes' Quest. I believe that inside, you are just as exceptional, able, principled and courageous as your most inspirational role models, from legend or from history, from sport, art or business. You inner hero or heroine is just waiting to be given permission to shine.

As we progress through this book we will look at how others have used similar skills and tools to do things that seemed impossible to them. Heroes, real or imagined, experience struggle or challenge just like you. Their tasks and goals were no less daunting than the mountain you want to climb, the dream job you want to win or the love you long to find. The difference however, is that they had a plan; a method for making their Quest a reality, something doable.

And that's what this book will share with you.

I am a big believer in the value of a practical skill set for managing your life. Whatever we want to achieve in life, having the tools to plan, organize and focus our activity is crucial. Most Quests also require a bit of research, the ability to lead, inspire or influence others and the confidence to stay in the game when things get tough. The skill set you will acquire through this book will help you to get comfortable with change. It will also give you a better understanding of who you are and how you operate so you can find the best ways to be useful and happy.

The Structure of Your Life Plan

We will begin by learning about the Heroes' Journey. This cycle is the foundation of every great story ever told. It follows a simple pattern of ups and downs, of resistance and action and offers a model to help us understand how life happens. Once we understand its structure, we can use it to inform how we operate in the world.

We will then take a look at who you are, in relation to your own Hero's Journey. We will explore how personality, motivations and talent entwine and give you clarity of purpose.

Once you have uncovered your Quest (whether big or small – some of the best Quests are known only to the hero in question – small can be very beautiful), we will move on to how you are going to get there. I will help you develop the project thinking you need to find the right people, process and plans to support you on the journey. I will show you how to build and lead a team, find mentors and champions and inspire others to join you. We will address the hero's nemeses – procrastination, doubt and fear – and you will discover how to break the patterns that keep you stuck and insecure. Together we will face the trials, tribulations and endurance tests that are part and parcel of transformation (and integral to any tale worth telling).

Out the other side, we will explore how to integrate your experience into the "new you" that emerges from the fire. You will also find ways to capture your experience and share it with others, so that you can be an inspiration and support to those that are struggling, stuck or feel that the Quest is out of their reach. This is the legacy of the Quest – once you have taken the journey, you are able to act as a light for others along the way.

As we progress through the book, I will introduce you to former clients, friends and colleagues who demonstrate the Heroes' Journey in action. We will hear stories from our real life heroes and heroines, as well as great examples from fiction to give us pointers about how Quests work. Each chapter will build your self-understanding, confidence and skill set and you will complete the book with a plan of action for your own unique Hero's Quest.

For the purposes of avoiding finger strain and the overuse of brackets, I am going to refer to "heroes" from now on. Heroines out there, know that I speak to you too, just in shorthand. The plentiful tales of kick-ass, inspirational women you will meet in these pages will back me up on that.

As meaning-making machines, human beings seek to live a life of purpose. We want to know why we are here, we want to make a difference, we want to leave a legacy; we want to grow, learn, evolve and overcome. Understanding the structure of our own life story can give us a method to understand why we are here and what we are here to do. It works for big and small dreams too and I encourage you to explore the upcoming ideas by starting small and testing them out for yourself.

Using This Book as a Group or Team

Your Life Plan is written directly to you, as an individual. However, it works equally well to support families, groups or teams to work on a shared goal. Just take the exercises and tools and run them as a discussion. No hero ever succeeds alone.

We live in uncertain and uncommon times. Times in which we recognize that the old goals and the old ways won't work for us. What has got us *here* won't get us *there*. And in uncertainty, our natural inclination is to stay safe, to not take risks or face too many challenges. But anything worth doing or having was always going to be a challenge. If it's not the economy, it's the lack of time. If it's not the lack of time it's that you aren't educated enough, hot enough, clever enough. Blah blah blah. Maybe you are tired of hearing all the reasons why it's not a good time to grab hold of your ambitions and your dreams. I hope that this book will help you navigate these challenges, stay calm and cool while you do it and give you the tools to create a better world.

Welcome to your life plan. Let the adventure begin!

1

THE HERO'S JOURNEY

" First they ignore you, then they laugh at you, then they fight you, then you win. *"*
Mahatma Gandhi

The art of a telling a good story is to keep the audience rapt and engaged – lost in the moment. There are a couple of skills that all storytellers have up their sleeves which will be really important for you to get to grips with to see yourself as the hero in your own life. The first skill is being able to recognize a polarity. The second is the ability to master and respect narrative flow.

The word "polarity" comes from the same root as the North and South Poles. A polarity means a contrast of opposites like hot and cold, dark and light or night and day. As human beings, our story-telling has focused on the contrast of good and evil, and love and loss. We recognize that to know what is good we must also know what is evil. To know happiness we must also know sorrow, one cannot make any sense of one without the other. We cannot always be happy, nor should we strive to be. When we look at any story of success, it always includes a period of doubt or of trial. This polarity is the nature of life and to avoid this is unhealthy. If we were always happy and had no polarity, life would be very boring indeed.

Have you noticed that all stories follow the same basic narrative? There is a beginning, a middle, and an end. We follow a character during a snapshot of their life. Sometimes their journey is tense and tight, at other times joyful and expansive. For example, the narrative flow of Shrek is broadly similar to that of James Bond. There is a universal structure to stories which doesn't change whether the tale is told by the fireside or as a 3D blockbuster at the local cinema. This chapter will introduce you to this secret story structure and help you align it with your own life experience. Once we know the rules in which we operate, we can begin to play a bigger game.

The Hero's Journey

Once, not all that long ago, there was an American professor called Joseph Campbell. Joseph was a professor of literature and one of the pre-eminent thinkers on myth and legend. He was an expert in stories and collected them from all over the world, examining them to find out what they had in common. From the fairy stories in the UK to the Green Man stories of Arabia, and from the religious tales of the Buddha to the teaching stories of the Aborigines, there was no storytelling tradition in the whole of the world that Joseph didn't know about. When he looked at all these tales, he found something very interesting. Everyone, everywhere, seemed to know what a hero or heroine was. And these heroes were the focus of all kinds of stories, of battle, of adventure, of love, of learning.

Not only that, everywhere you went in the world, people also knew what a "Hero's Quest" was. The idea of going on a great journey, undertaking challenges and coming back transformed by your experience. Wherever you were in the world, local people recognized what a Quest involved.

The most interesting thing he learned was that really, when you looked at it, there was only ONE story. In all the stories from different cultures, belief systems and heroes, the essential structure of the tale told about the hero was the same. Because there was only one story, Joseph called this structure the "monomyth." The myth from which all other tales are derived. This structure eventually became known as "The Hero's Journey."

Why is this relevant to us, here in the real world, I hear you cry? Well, apart from the fact that this structure makes for a super story, the Hero's Journey relates not just to fantasy and imaginary characters, but to REAL ones. This structure is actually a map for HOW LIFE HAPPENS. Once you can read this map, you are in a much stronger place to understand where you are in the process of change. We have a tendency to think that when things get hard, we are in the wrong place. We become uncomfortable. We want to stop or give up. We become disorientated. When you know where you are and appreciate that the polarity of easy/hard, strong/weak, lost/found is in operation, you can feel a lot more relaxed about the journey, knowing you are exactly where you should be and pressing on until the polarity in your story changes.

Not one to take things as given, I tested this idea out. Is it really true that anyone, anywhere can understand the Hero's Journey and relate it to their own feelings and their own lives? I have now run workshops on this model for seven years sharing these ideas with hundreds of people across several continents here in the UK, in India, New Zealand, the USA and Kosovo. Every single person who I showed it to, from the very young to the very old, could relate it to their lives and experience.

Let's take a look at the structure. To help us, let's call on one of the best-loved cinematic stories ever told. The original *Star Wars*. In developing what was to become a film classic, George Lucas hired Joseph Campbell as a consultant to give him advice on the monomyth. No doubt the special effects, the whopping budget and some marvellous acting helped to make the film such a success. But it was the Hero's Journey structure that made it possible to create such a memorable film. Lucas claimed that he knew the pieces of what made a classic tale, but wasn't clear about the order they came in or how to make the most of them. *Star Wars* combines many of the key elements of great storytelling – the hero we can relate to, enjoyable and likeable sidekicks, the rescue of a princess, the defeat of evil and the surprising turn of events. Let's look in more detail at what Campbell and Lucas created as we break down the Hero's Journey.

The Headlines of the Hero's Journey – the Path to the Quest

Part One – the Call

The hero is looking for something – either to leave an unsuitable situation or to move toward an exciting dream or goal. But they feel stuck. They know there is more out there for them – they want to stretch beyond the known, but it feels frightening. Then one day, for whatever reason, they are "Called" – something happens that makes them decide they must commit and take action. This usually takes quite a bit of courage.

> Luke Skywalker is cleaning the robot R2-D2 when he accidentally triggers a hidden message from Princess Leia, who has been kidnapped by Darth Vader. The message begs for help and rescue. When Luke visits Obi-Wan Kenobi to tell him about the message, he asks about his father – who is he? Luke is now "Called" to rescue the princess.

Part Two – the Commitment

The hero crosses the threshold into the unknown. They leave behind what is familiar and commit to their Quest. In this time they receive support, mentoring and assistance. They make a plan and pull together the resources to get started.

> Luke hires Hans Solo and Chewbacca to transport him to Alderaan, Leia's home world. Obi-wan Kenobi serves as his mentor and sidekick.

Part Three – the Quest

The Belly of the Whale: It gets dark and lonely, the hero feels lost. They wonder why they ever started and if they can ever complete their Quest. There are tests and trials that prove they are up to the Quest.

The Supreme Ordeal: They face a final battle or challenge that is often life threatening, or they do battle with their own limitations or fears. The hero's commitment and integrity is put to the test.

> Obi-Wan Kenobi gets killed in a battle with Darth Vader. He makes the ultimate sacrifice to help the higher cause. Luke faces Darth Vader, in a great lightsaber duel and Darth reveals that he is Luke's father attempting to lure him to the Dark Side (Belly of the Whale). Luke returns to Yoda (his mentor) to complete his training and it is revealed that he will have to face his father to become a true Jedi. He discovers that Leia is his sister. A final battle ensues (Supreme Ordeal) and Luke overpowers Darth, but refrains from killing him. His father then saves him in a final act of heroism before he dies.

Part Four – the Return

Transformed by their experience, the heroic character needs time to recover. They then return across the threshold back into the "ordinary" world, able to share the gifts and wisdom they have accumulated through their Heroes' Journey. They are greeted with great joy and fanfare.

> Anakin Skywalker (aka Darth Vader) dies in his son's arms. Luke graduates to become a Jedi Knight and the Death Star is destroyed. Luke returns home, a very different man to the one who began the Quest.

This structure can be found in any of the religious stories, fairy tales, in Disney and in Dickens. Writers have used it for centuries. Why? Because it echoes our own life experience. The Heroes' Journey is the structure of our life – when we change and learn, we move from highs to lows, from confidence to anxiety and we have to be persistent, against all odds or face giving up on our dreams.

My grandmother was born in Russia and in spite of being a Jewish woman in a Communist state, became a very successful physicist. She loved her job. She was the only woman in Russia responsible for a scientific institute. But she, her husband, her mother and her son, dreamed of the freedom they might have if they lived in the West. Her husband, my grandfather, had lost his whole family in World War II in Poland. He was a Zionist and wanted the family to move to Israel where they could live safe from persecution. The family took the opportunity to apply to leave Russia. This was their Call. Everyone applied, steadily going through the paperwork and bureaucracy that was designed by the Communist regime to wear you down and make you give up. They waited and waited. The answer finally came back; only my father, her son, had permission to leave. The rest of the family were now "traitors" to the regime. There was a family conference and they agreed that my father, who was only 21 years old, would leave Russia. He began his own Hero's Quest that took him to Israel and then to England.

Life now became very difficult for my grandparents. My grandmother lost the job she loved. One day shortly after my father left, she went to work and there was someone else sitting at her desk. She was barred from the building and the world of work. My grandfather was accused of "making up" his medals won for courageous fighting on behalf of the Soviets. They were exiled from their country whilst still living there. With nowhere to go and in the Belly of the Whale, my grandmother joined the resistance movement, the Refuseniks, a community of activists who had been refused permission to leave Russia. She fought for the rights of others to leave the country, was arrested by the KGB and often did not know whether she would "disappear." Those were terrible times for my father, not least because my grandfather and my great-grandmother died during that time. Finally, after much campaigning and strain, my grandmother was able to leave. She, like my father before, had to leave almost everything behind, go to a strange country and start life all over again. She brought with her her courage, her expertise and her eccentricity. She is one of my heroes. Her story stands for me, for others and for anyone who has had to leave everything behind to be free.

Finding Your Direction

The Hero's Journey is our roadmap for life. Life is always giving us opportunities to respond and stretch and grow. There are Calls happening in our lives all the time. How we respond to the challenges helps us better understand who we are. As we deal with the challenges along the way, we shape who we are and we grow into a fuller version of ourselves. A bit like a snake shedding its skin as it outgrows it, we retain the basic essence of ourselves and we discard the life and habits that we have outgrown and no longer need.

When you look at your own life, where can you see the pattern of a Hero's Journey? Where have you outgrown an old skin, a place, a way of being and explored something altogether new?

Have you ever:

- Moved house?
- Had a family?
- Been in love?
- Ended a relationship?
- Started a new job? Left an old one?
- Started a business or a campaign?
- Passed an exam?
- Grown your own fruit or vegetables?
- Learned a new skill or hobby from scratch?
- Lived or travelled somewhere new?

All of these life changes and transitions constitute a Heroes' Journey.

Going Deeper

When we allow ourselves to believe that *our lives* follow the same story structure as the classic heroic Quest story, we can begin to use this structure to make sense of our experience. If we cultivate the qualities and characteristics of successful heroes, this could help us develop and follow through on the kinds of plans that change our whole lives.

So, let's get into the detail of the four different stages of the Hero's Journey which make up the four main parts of this book.

Part One – the Call

Brrrring, Brrring.

"Hello?"

"Quick! I need a hero!"

OK, so it may not happen exactly like the above phone call. It might be a text message, an email, a whisper, something you hear on the radio, something you read that inspires you; but somehow inside of you, something starts to shift. You begin to imagine a great goal or achievement, something you really want. Or you may decide that you won't allow something negative that has been going on for a long time to continue. We could say that being motivated to get rid of something is like a *push*, and being motivated to get something we do want, feels more like a *pull*. So the Call is a push or a pull that moves you in the direction of something different and inspires you to start on a journey. Examples of this might be:

- You decide you want to learn guitar/a language/a new sport.
- You decide that you want to work in a new field.
- You decide it is time to start a family.
- You decide that you will stop being a doormat in relationships or at work.
- You decide to get fit/get healthy/stop smoking/tackle an addiction.
- You decide to leave a job/relationship/life that is no longer working for you.

- You decide to launch a magazine/DJ on the radio/start a charity/launch a campaign/start a business.

Sometimes we may resist a Call because even if we know that something would be a great thing to do, we don't want to be told to do it by someone else. Or we feel like what we are proposing is unrealistic, or not normal, or even impossible. We may be scared what the effects of the change might be in our lives or what other people might say or think. We are often held back by our own fear of failure. Sometimes change just seems plain inconvenient, awkward or uncomfortable.

Sooner or later though, a Call comes along that you just cannot resist. Either it becomes too painful to continue in a relationship/job/body/lifestyle that is not working, or you become overwhelmed by the feeling that if you don't give what you are dreaming of a try, you will regret it for the whole of your life. Once the Call is inside you, once the seed has been sown, it just keeps on coming up again and again until you throw in the towel and say "OK, I am going to give it a try." And that's when the magic starts to happen.

Part One will help you unlock your motivation, discover your talents and learn to hear your Call. We will address how to uncover your Quest and how to make the decision to commit.

Part Two – the Commitment: Letting Go of the Certain and Stepping into the New

" And the day came when the risk
to remain tight in a bud was more
painful than the risk it took to blossom. *"*
Anaïs Nin

Accepting the Call means stepping into the unknown. It is Eve eating the apple. Once it is done, it cannot be undone. To do this, we need to step through our fear, the concerns and anxieties of those around us and the "practical and logical" limitations that seem to keep us bound to what is familiar and safe. As we work through the resistance and keep moving forward, we finally reach the jumping-off point. This is the point where we leave the normal and enter a world of magic and extraordinary potential. When we allow ourselves to jump, the world seems to come up to meet us. Have you seen the scene in the film *Indiana Jones and the Last Crusade* where he has to take a step into nothingness and a bridge suddenly appears below his feet? That's what we are aiming for. To step out with faith, cross the threshold and trust that the world will "rise up" to meet us.

This is arguably the most feel-good part of the Hero's Journey. There's something very powerful that happens when you make a commitment and take a really firm decision. Somehow, support, help and encouragement come around you to help you to succeed. David, who is just 14, gave me a great example of this:

> "I'd always loved markets. Ever since I was a kid, I used to go to the Sunday markets and car boot sales, just to look at the huge range of stuff you could get there. My dad suggested that I open a stall. At first, I wasn't too sure. It seemed like there was a lot of organization involved and anyway, I didn't know what I could sell. But then I came across this website for a warehouse not so far from my town, where you could buy all kinds of cheap games and toys and tricks. It was like a light bulb went off in my mind. I got really excited about having the best mini-toy stall in town. After I decided to do it, my nan offered me £50 to buy my first stock and the community centre youth workers offered me a table and cash tin. And my best mate promised to help me organize it and to set up and sell on the day . . . and suddenly I was in business!"

When you say yes to the Call, weird stuff starts happening. You start to find the things you need to succeed in your Quest. People, resources, support and skills come into your life with surprising ease. It's as though the world conspires to help you make the vision of yourself that your Quest symbolizes a reality.

Think about David. When he said yes to his market stall, he got money for stock and the kit he needed for his stall. Harry Potter got an owl, a wand and – crucially – some allies to help him along the way, Hermione and Ron. Accepting the Call is a time of positive energy and good support. In Part Two, The Commitment, we will explore how to step through resistance, "initiate" ourselves into our Quest and take our first steps into this brave new world.

Part Three – the Quest: Getting Going, Getting Lost and Getting Through

The start of the Quest looks a lot like the montage action training scenes you get in big-screen action movies. It's the "time is passing and we are arming up for a great adventure" bit. In Part Three we get into the practical realities of being on a Quest and I show you how to make a plan, align other people around your vision and use the energy that comes with the start of your Quest to take positive action, explore, try new things and get results.

Belly of the Whale: Getting Lost

The name of this part of the Hero's Journey refers to the story of Jonah in the Bible. Jonah is thrown into the sea during a storm and a whale comes and swallows him up. As you can imagine, the belly of a whale is not a nice place to be – dark and smelling strongly of decomposing fish. Jonah is not happy at all. This is the time when the doubt sets in. Having found friends and mentors, the hero has set off on the journey and as time goes on, the path gets lonelier and darker. They lose confidence, their commitment is tested, perhaps they even lose their way and forget why they ever started on their Quest. This is a difficult and challenging time, which often occurs when we are working hard to master something or to get somewhere, but wonder if we will ever make it.

Imagine the long years spent training by a rower for the Olympics – breaking the ice at five o'clock in the morning on the Thames you must wonder – is this really worth it? What if I am wasting my time? This stage of our life journey teaches us about determination, focus, planning and calling on the support of those around us.

I am sure that there have been times in your life when you have been in this position. You began something with energy and enthusiasm, then as time went on, you lost your focus. Everything took a thousand times longer than you had hoped. Did you keep going? How did you find the will to do so?

The Supreme Ordeal

" Changes are the products of intensive efforts. *"*
Muhammad Yunus, founder of the Grameen Bank

A hero story wouldn't be a great story without some kind of supreme challenge or battle. The things we really want in life don't come easily and they often require the star of the story to stretch further than they ever thought they could. We love this part of a story, whether it is a real life one or a fantasy tale. Think about reality TV for a moment. Love it or hate it, there is always a tense battle for places in the final and we become emotionally involved, rooting for our favourites to win. For a football team, this could be the final game, for a student with dreams of going to drama school, it could be the audition. For an amateur celebrity dancer, it could be winning the TV competition, *Strictly Come Dancing*. For Harry Potter, it is always an encounter with Voldemort.

The Supreme Ordeal is the ultimate test, the baptism of fire we need to endure in order to have a breakthrough. It is the facing of our fears, the lifting of the curtain, it is show time, the birthing table, the battle.

These are the times when our emotional resources, courage and wisdom are really put to the test. Part Three of the book explores how to prepare for and handle the Grand Challenge stage, giving you tools to stay positive and determined when the terrain gets really rough.

Part Four – the Return

Post-battle, every hero needs a little downtime. Time to reflect on what has happened, regroup and return to the world you came from a little different from when you started. Will Luke Skywalker ever be the same after discovering Darth Vader is his father? He's going to need a bit of time to integrate the learning from his experience into his life again. The same is true for the recovery stage of our own Heroes' Journey. At the end of *The Lord of the Rings*, Frodo is taken to the Undying Lands to recover as best he can. Most probably, after you have run the marathon, got over the big shock, worked hard to make your first gig/theatre production/invention a success, you will need to relax and to explore how you might have been changed by the experience. Later in the book, we will explore the idea of how to learn lessons from reflecting on what has happened to you and use these to grow as a person.

Every great story ends with the hero returning to a great welcome – the Hunchback of Notre Dame went from being a scary monster hiding in the shadows to the saviour of Paris, Harry's return to Hogwarts after a battle is always met with elation from his fellow students. The hero is transformed by their experience – they have grown richer, wiser, deeper and they return with the victory or the learning or the gifts that they then share with others around them.

Real life is not always like fairy stories or the world of Disney. We lack the happy ending. Our Supreme Ordeal leaves us worn down. Even a seemingly happy ending like a windfall lottery win can create as many problems as opportunities.

Or perhaps we don't receive the recognition we may deserve or crave. Rosalind Franklin's work was crucial to the discovery of DNA, but it was Watson and Crick who took the glory. The lessons in the quiet downtime after battle can be just as valuable to us as a glorious fanfare. Part Four will help you to integrate the lessons of your Quest in a way that makes them valuable, even when the outcome looks rather different from what you had planned.

Whatever the result, the learning from your adventure will need to be integrated, consolidated and shared. Part Four also explores the importance of marking and recognizing your transition, returning from a state of heightened reality to "normal" life and how to package your learning so that you can share it with others.

These experiences will enable you to do and think differently.

Experience is always our greatest teacher.

So this Hero's Journey is a model for the way life works. Hopefully now you can see how this model both relates to good storytelling and is a way to understand the transformations and choices we may be called to make in our own lives.

- How does it feel to know that it is normal to struggle with a decision or choice that seems too big to achieve?
- Or that once you have set out on your way it is part of the process to feel a bit lost?
- Or that we all face battles and challenges that are on a grand scale and sometimes we have to encounter them again and again before we get to the other side?

We will be using this model to explore the kinds of feelings and situations that come up in your Hero's Quest. But before we can work with these, we need to find out a bit more about you and the way you work.

 Chapter Summary

- The contrasts of story and the narrative flow of the Hero's Journey make sense to us because they mirror how life happens.

- We see this structure in operation in great fiction as well as in real life.

- Each stage of the journey has a distinct flavour and quality.

- When we understand this narrative, it helps us to cope with "how life happens."

- We can use the Hero's Journey as a way to structure our thinking about our own goals, dreams and Quests.

2

WHAT KIND OF HERO ARE YOU ANYWAY?

II Intelligence is composed mostly
of imagination and insight, things
that have nothing to do with reason. *II*
Vivienne Westwood

The Hero's Journey gives us a model to understand how change happens in our lives. What we next need to find out about is the central character in the story – you – your history, character and desires. Being your own hero does not mean you need to be perfect. Every hero comes with flaws and challenges. They all need help and support from others with other gifts.

Being a hero is about embodying the best version of yourself. If you can learn how to harness your own talents, you can "play a larger game" and become exceptional in your field. This chapter is about the process of self-discovery. Here we will identify your talents and motivations so that you can find the environments and opportunities that help you grow, and use these abilities to the full.

The exercises set out in this chapter enable you to discover the hero inside of you and we will explore and uncover the unique configuration that makes yourself, well, "selfey." We will be uncovering your skill set, your intelligences and your personality type. By the end, you will be able to confidently answer the question, "So what do you bring to the party?"

No one is perfect. Not in real life. John McEnroe played great tennis and had an awful temper with it. Oprah Winfrey has lifted and inspired millions of people and championed valuable humanitarian causes, but struggles to maintain her weight and manage her eating. Einstein was a genius but was an utter nightmare to live with. You do not need to be perfect to have a profound influence on the world. You do not need to strive for perfection. You can make a small change or move toward a little dream and achieve it and deserve it because you are you. And you are enough.

To do this we need to have a good understanding of who we are. Human beings do not come with a manual. This means we have to get curious and figure out our operating system, benefits and features. We can go through many years of our lives without knowing what a particular button does on our radio. The same is true for ourselves. Until each of us is born with a manual, or scientists learn to navigate the variations in our brains to tell us all about who we are, we are going to need to do some self-exploration of our own.

If we can get a better grasp of our motivations, skills and "type" then we can make better of use of these things to help us achieve our life goals and fulfil our Quests. We can also share what we know of ourselves with others, helping to minimize misunderstanding, build mutual appreciation and tolerance, and make better choices all round.

Here are the key aspects of self we will explore:

1. Your Heroes and their Qualities
2. Your Unique Features
3. Your Intelligences
4. Your Values
5. Your Risk Profile
6. Your "Fit"

These ingredients will enable you to build your own self-awareness guide. You will then be ready to explore your Quest and will be in a good place to take the plunge into the Commitment stage of the journey. In life and within the Western education system, we are all too often pushed into decisions concerning our future, our careers, our next steps, without this grounding in who we are. So no skipping this chapter, it's the foundation of your Quest.

The Good News

A dear friend sent me this postcard during the "mad cow disease" epidemic in the 1990s:

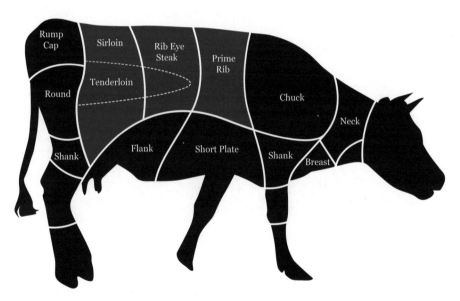

"I may not be perfect but parts of me are excellent."

Today, you get to be the cow!

There are going to be things that you are brilliant at. You may know about them already or they may be lying in wait for you to discover them. I am a great storyteller and I can translate complicated ideas into simple and practical tools for people to use in their lives. This is my zone of "brilliance." We all have one and although I have a natural aptitude, I have also put the hours in. They say it takes 10,000 hours to become a master at something. That's five years full-time work. If you want to be great at something, you are going to need to turn up and do the work – and if you have chosen something you have an aptitude for, you are likely to be successful. So the mindset is – be honest with yourself, be kind and be balanced. I want you to focus on discovering your strengths and then mastering them.

The Bad News

II It is the most shattering experience of a young man's life when one morning he awakes and quite reasonably says to himself 'I will *never* play the Dane.' When that moment comes, one's ambition ceases. *II*
Uncle Monty, Withnail and I *written by Bruce Robinson*

Discovering your heroic profile is about getting real and recognizing your limitations and your capabilities. Of course, I want you to challenge yourself, to stretch beyond what is comfortable, to surprise yourself. But, I also will not allow you to set yourself up to fail. We will look at how to work out whether we have capability in something or whether we are now using this book to skive off or duck out of making our dreams come true.

For example, I will never be a world-class athletics champion. I have left it too late in life. I have rather short legs and I'm mildly allergic to running. I don't have great motor intelligence. It takes me ages to learn to do anything that involves translating a thought into a physical action – like learning to drive. Eventually I passed my driving test, but it took me three attempts and it doesn't stop my other half imitating tyre-squealing noises whenever I drive round a corner!

Anyway, the point is, you just simply don't need to be good at everything to have a great life.

Everyone has their own set of gifts. Each and every person is very able in some areas and less so in others. We each have a unique range of skills that our manual, if we had one, would call our "features." These features suit some Quests more than others. So I, Erica, am built for writing, speaking and digesting information, not for science, calculations, auditing or anything that requires decent spatial awareness – what are you built for?

Let's find out.

1. Your Heroes and Their Qualities

Heroes, protagonists, activists – whatever you want to call them, the hero is someone that we are inspired by. Heroic characters show us what is possible in life. They stand for what they believe in. They do things their own way. They think independently. They take risks to achieve their goals. They are resilient. They call in support from other people to help them achieve something that is important to them. Our choice of heroes is very personal. Each of us will have qualities we admire in ourselves, and each of us will be influenced by characters from real life or fiction, whose stories reflect something important for us.

Uncovering the heroic qualities that you most value

- Identify the people who inspire you the most. They can be friends and family, well known or anonymous, alive or dead, from fantasy or from history and from any walk of life.
- As you write their names down, have a go at identifying what qualities they possess that you most admire.

  My list as an example; alongside my grandmother, my heroes include:
  - Dad – brave, independent, loyal
  - Tori Amos – quirky, talented, eccentric, independent, unique
  - Vivienne Westwood – strong, creative, passionate, her own woman
  - Freddie Mercury – charismatic, creative, did what he did excellently, strong drive, entertaining
  - Anaïs Nin – unconventional, free, creative, prolific, wise
- Look closely at your list. Are there particular themes, behaviours or character traits in there that you most value?
- Now ask yourself – what would life be like if you expressed these qualities more in your own life? Are you willing to do so?

Living a heroic life, expanding into all you can be, means being willing to grow into these qualities. Your Quest will invite you to practice living more of your life with these qualities at the forefront. If these qualities feel like "achey" muscles, they will need some re-training.

What action could you take to build the expression of these qualities?

2. Your Unique Features

In marketing speak, a fact about a product is known as a "feature." This is something that products possess, for example, every car has wheels. Marketers also talk about the benefits – the advantages that the feature offers. In the case of the car, it would be getting to my grandma's house in Golders Green much faster than if I walked.

When features and benefits marry nicely, they offer a great solution to a problem. Take a spork – the great camping cutlery invention.

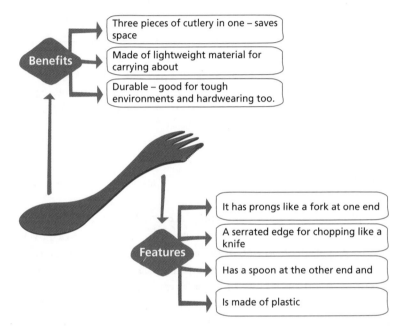

The design of a spork is perfectly matched to accomplish the task it needs to perform (eating) and the environments in which we are going to perform that task (by a fire in the woods). We want to discover your features and benefits so that you can start to identify what you are designed for.

 Brainstorm all of the design features you possess that you value. Set your timer for 60 seconds. Don't pause, don't hesitate, anything you value counts. Ready, steady . . . go!

How did you do? Was it easy to describe yourself and your abilities? Was it hard to be generous? Sometimes it can feel very uncomfortable to name and describe our abilities. We often get told that claiming who you are and being confident about being who you are is arrogance, bragging, or in some other way undesirable. To help counteract this shaming, let's look at you from another angle – from the perspective of those who care about you.

 Set the timer. Think of someone in your life who really cares about you – a partner, a friend, a parent, a sibling, a teacher who really saw who you are. What would they describe as your unique features? What do they value? Set the timer for 60 seconds. Ready, steady . . . go!

Oh, go on with you . . .

Compliments that mean something are another great shortcut to uncovering your unique features. One of my favourites was given to me by a student on one of my enterprise courses. Lyndsey runs a great little online gardening business called What You Sow (www.whatyousow.co.uk) offering gardening gift ideas to make growing a lovely experience. She told me: "The thing I love about the way you teach Erica, is that everyone gets to learn from one another. You allow space and time for the group to share information and you draw out the learning from our business experiences. So each of us feels like an expert."

What features about how I teach did Lyndsey capture?

Features

- I put a group of (normally isolated) entrepreneurs together in one place.
- I create space and structure talk and share ideas.
- I ask good questions.

Benefits

- Create a great learning environment.
- Bring people together.
- Help to facilitate good conversations.
- Build confidence.

Now you have a go.

- What's the best compliment anyone has ever paid you?
- Which of your design features did it highlight?
- What are the benefits of those features?
- Now have a think back to what you were doing to generate the compliment. Was that an activity or communication that you were really proud of? How did you feel when you were doing it?
- Where and What contexts can you imagine that someone with those features and benefits might be useful?
- To whom could those design features and benefits be useful?
- How much are you using those abilities and skills at the moment? (give it a percentage)
- How do you feel knowing this?

Being in Your Element

Ken Robinson, an expert in creativity and education, describes the activities that we love to do as "being in our element." He emphasizes the importance of discovering our sphere of excellence and passion. To embark on a Quest, you will need to know as much as you can about the abilities required to carry it through. You will also need to make sure that your Quest can help you to be more of yourself, express more of who you are or grow your ability to flow in the face of challenge.

Your element may seem to you to be something quite small – yet exercising it can bring great joy to yourself and to those who are touched by it.

Remember, people make a living out of the zaniest things: making people laugh, icing fancy cupcakes, creating surprising shapes with their bodies and tasting fine wine. Whilst you may not want to create a career out of your element, discovering what that is for you can be very valuable when you pull together your tool bag for your Quest.

So, here is an exercise to uncover your element. The thing you cannot stop doing. The thing you would do whether you were paid for it or not. The natural and innate skill set that you possess. When you explore this exercise, I want you to be really specific and detailed. So if you love to do sudoku puzzles, dig down into that. What is it about them that you love? Overcoming a challenge? Making them add up? Solving a problem? Completing something? The more specific you can be, the more useful this exercise will be to you.

- What do you love to do?
- What have you been told you have a real gift for?
- What can you not stop doing, even if it isn't your business or is the wrong time of day?
- What would you describe as your passion? (You know this because if there is an article about it, or an ad, or something on the radio or TV, you will always stop to notice it, amongst the cacophony of images and messages we are exposed to every day.)
- How could you bring your element into more frequent day-to-day use?

A note to the world weary; I will not buy the idea that it is "too late" to discover yourself and your talents. Research from the British Career Advice Service suggests over half of the over fifties would still like to find and try their dream job. Take the lawyer who in his late sixties has recently been accepted at Nottingham to study medicine. Many of my coachees have been surprised to discover "latent talents" later in life. A latent talent is something that you have a natural gift for, but never used, so the talent lay dormant. This is the strongest argument I have to encourage you to keep breaking new ground. Try new things, eat new food, take an unusual class. You might surprise yourself. My other half is 56 and has spent his professional career in software engineering, and his personal life climbing mountains and sailing seas. He recently enrolled on an Art Foundation course with a bunch of teenagers. His appreciation of detail and his patience and determination are combining with his latent talent for drawing. His future is bright. So with him and you in mind, let's do one more exercise for latent talents – those things you have a hunch you would be great at, but have yet to try.

- What have you always longed to try, but never yet found the time?
- What makes you think you would like it?
- How do you think trying it would make you feel?
- Complete the sentence: if there were no restrictions on me and I could easily afford it I would spend my time . . .

What action are you now willing to take to spend more of your time in your element?

This is the skill set you want to play to. Our passions give us joy and we are often blessed with the skills to do a great job on them. If you work in an area of your passion, or express it in a hobby or free-time activity, you are gifting yourself with a moment of fun and play and who doesn't deserve more of that?

Heroes in their element have learned to play to their strengths – they play where they can have an impact, learn more, be useful and have fun. And they also do their best to avoid too much time in the tasks and skill sets that they don't have a real talent for. Instead, they find team members who are exceptional in their area of weakness and collaborate with them. This can take some time. Not everyone has the confidence, clarity or situation that makes it easy to refuse to do anything that does not align with their skill set, design and passions.

Musician Max Fraser, also known as Maxi Jazz, worked at BT for several years before deciding to heed the Call and really focus on his music career. Eight years later, this decision led to the formation of the band Faithless, who went on to sell over 15 million albums worldwide. Here, he talks about the courage it took to leave the security of this job:

> "I called my job terminal cancer of the soul. There are many kinds of death but that was the one I feared the most. The one where you stop being yourself because of the environment you are in. What motivated me to leave was the horrifying idea that I could wake up at 65 only having worked at BT. I was smart enough to realize at 29 that I couldn't just up and leave. I didn't expect it to take overnight, but I didn't expect it to take three years either."

To make space for your element, you will need to stop doing some things that don't give you the feeling of flow. Be honest now. We all have to do things we don't like – cleaning the house, putting things away, paying the bills. But we also waste a lot of our time on pointless, mindless, numbing distractions instead of living a life that helps us discover more about ourselves, brings our childlike curiosity out and expresses something positive. So come on, out with it.

- What do you need to stop doing?
- Is there anything going on in your life that might be eating at you in a "cancer of the soul" fashion?

3. Your Intelligences

> **"** I want my children to understand the world, but not just because the world is fascinating and the human mind is curious. I want them to understand it so that they will be positioned to make it a better place . . . An important part of that understanding is knowing who we are and what we can do. **"**
> *Howard Gardner*

Every superhero has a unique and special power or talent. In the NBC show, *Heroes*, these included: the cheerleader who could repair her injured body, a politician who could fly, a police officer who could read people's minds and an addict who could paint the future. While our talent list may not extend to the realms of fantasy, we too have variable levels of aptitude in different types of smarts and so another way of getting to know your skill set is to explore the "type" of intelligence you have. The education system doesn't always value or differentiate between these intelligences. It focuses assessment on a very narrow range of skill sets mostly involving memory, fact retention and some problem solving. So it can be easy for us to go through life believing we are not intelligent in the traditional sense, yet have many other forms of intelligent ability.

Howard Gardner is an American academic. "Multiple intelligences" was a term coined by him. Howard has dedicated much of his life's work to uncovering and naming the intelligences. I've set them out below for you. Take time to scan through them and then identify your top three.

- **Spatial intelligence** – the ability to recognize and gracefully work within space and to use this intelligence to navigate in more compact areas (like parallel parking for instance).

- **Interpersonal intelligence** – the ability to understand the intentions, motivations and desires of other people. It allows people to work effectively with others and build relationships.
- **Linguistic intelligence** – the ability to understand and use language to accomplish goals or express oneself. We use this skill set when marketing a business, speaking in public or writing an article.
- **Logical/mathematical intelligence** – the ability to analyze, investigate and use logic to solve problems.
- **Musical intelligence** – the ability to spot patterns that create harmony, melody and pitch and to translate these into compositions.
- **Intrapersonal intelligence** – the ability to look inside and understand oneself, to appreciate one's feelings, fears and motivations.
- **Bodily-kinesthetic intelligence** – the ability to use our bodies or parts of the body to overcome obstacles or tackle a particular physical challenges.
- **Naturalist intelligence** – the ability to recognize, categorize and make use of information relating to the natural environment.
- **Moral intelligence** – the ability to focus upon and prioritize the rules, behaviours and attitudes that govern the sanctity of life and wellbeing of all living creatures and the world they inhabit.

What are your top three natural intelligences?
- 1.
- 2.
- 3.

Now review the list again for the one or two that you know you struggle with a little more. When you think about your Quest over the next few chapters, you will want to be on the lookout for tasks that require this kind of intelligence and begin to think about who or what could support you in completing those tasks.

In a way it doesn't matter whether we agree with the categories that Gardner has given us. What his work does is help us to under-stand our uniqueness – each of us has numerous strengths across these general categories. The more specific we can get about which ones "feel" like us, the more we can use this to guide our sense of our own heroism.

For more information about Howard Gardner and to find out where to take the intelligence test, please check out the resource section at the end of this book.

4. Your Values

Think about a boat bobbing about on the ocean. It might sway left and right with the tide and the waves, but if it has an anchor attached, this will prevent it drifting off and getting lost at sea. Our values are like our anchors – they tie us to who we are in a way that rarely changes throughout our lives. Our values are our guiding principles, the criteria against which we make decisions and the aspects of life that we most prize. In our teens, we tend to rebel against the values of our parents or caregivers, it's a natural part of the self-differentiation stage. However, in the long term, we do tend to align to the values that we grew up with.

Take a moment to look at the values you were taught as a young person. For me, with parents as first-generation immigrants, educa-tion was a key value. The ideas of working hard, learning new things, becoming accomplished, these values were drummed into me at almost every key decision point in my life. Rightly or wrongly, my parents wanted me to have the best education they could afford and they expected me to put the effort in to justify the expense. I also watched my parents work very hard to create financial stabil-ity for themselves, with my father doing two or three jobs when I was very young. I learned that autonomy and independence were important and these have remained guiding forces in my life. So it is no surprise that I have found myself working in the education field, always learning new things and often working in an independent fashion – either as a freelancer or as a change agent in a business.

- Rightly or wrongly, what did your parents teach you to value?
- What principles guided their lives and decisions?
- Which of these still resonate with you today?
- Are there other values that you have learned to prize – when and how did these become important to you?

We are not our parents. They gave us our lives, but we need to claim *our* life and live by what matters to us. Our parents did the best they could with the knowledge and skill set they had at the time. Part of our growing up is realizing that we have choices about which of the gifts they gave us we wish to take with us and which we wish to leave behind.

5. Your Risk Profile

If you have ever been involved in a pension or investment discussion, the concept of a risk "profile" will not be foreign to you. For everyone else, any time you decide to take on an activity or responsibility about which you are not supremely confident, you are in the process of managing risk. Risk is defined by the *Oxford Dictionary* as "to expose oneself to danger and harm."

Risk is relevant in almost every aspect of our lives. Trevor Baylis, inventor of the wind-up radio once described us as "a banana skin away from serious injury." Luckily, most of us are not conscious of risk all the time; if we were, we would be a very worried bunch indeed. However, anything that you want to try that you haven't done before will raise your risk antennae. This helps your survival instinct make an assessment of whether your next move will seriously harm your health.

Although many life projects can be started without a serious risk assessment, there are also many where your level of comfort around risk will be important.

If, for example, you are looking to take on a business or go self-employed, you will need to be comfortable with a certain measure of financial exposure, which if things do not go according to plan, may leave you in a precarious position in relation to money. Or if you are about to begin a significant physical challenge, like breaking a world record for sailing round the world, then you may need to consider the risk of doing damage to yourself when you assess the strain of the challenge.

Here are the three levels of risk that a pension adviser would typically assess you on concerning your finances. We can use these to determine your level of risk in general life.

1. A High risk tolerance means that you are comfortable with narrow odds, don't mind a significant fail, fall or loss, feel yourself to be resilient and would call yourself a bit of a gambler.
2. A Medium risk tolerance means that you can take moderate risks, in a variety of circumstances, but do not like to leave things too much to chance – you are willing to take a calculated risk if you feel it could pay off.
3. A Low risk tolerance means that you are not comfortable with much that is outside your sphere of control and expertise. You would rather take a low guaranteed return than chance your hand at something that you are not confident will deliver.

Which one sounds most like you?

If you are job hunting, you will begin to notice that some jobs – investment trading, commission-only sales, are more risky than others. If you are considering a project that means a lot to you but may not be a success, e.g. restoring an old boat or property, having a child through IVF, then you may wish to consider whether your next step is in line with your risk level. Our later exploration of the support you may need in your life project should be useful for toning up your risk and resilience muscle. You will learn how to bounce back as well as prepare yourself to respond effectively to unexpected surprises.

6. Your "Fit"

The final factor to consider when reflecting on your Quest is the context in which you are most likely to be successful. Do you need people around you in a team, or do you prefer to work alone? Are you someone who likes a structure set by a mentor or expert, or do you prefer to devise your own programme? Do you want to be a parent to a child regardless of whether you have a partner or not, or do you only fantasize about a family with A.N. Other?

These things are important. Sometimes it is a matter of trial and error. You can only know that an environment does not suit you by trying it out. For me, for example, I love working with ideas and their practical application – especially in relation to people's lives. My first role was as a policy adviser at the Home Office. I was dealing with interesting topics, such as sex offending and corporate manslaughter and I loved the variety of the job. But the inherent conservatism of the Civil Service and the snail-like pace it moved at used to drive me batty! I got bored, frustrated, fidgety, demanding. I didn't feel I was really making a difference in people's lives. So when I was offered an alternative opportunity that was more about individual people's lives, I grabbed it and was much, much happier in that role. Trying to fit yourself as a square peg into a round hole can cause all kinds of health problems, lead to stress, anxiety and "failure."

A Fresh Approach

Sometimes you are also in the right sphere but approaching it in the wrong way. Karen worked for a language lessons franchise.

Karen is a single parent and was recently made redundant so it was really important that the next move she made worked financially for her and her daughter. When she told me about the marketing efforts she had put in, Karen seemed really glum. We very quickly established that the sums just didn't add up. Then she told me the other franchisees weren't doing so well either. Then we got on to the fact that although she enjoyed teaching the children, working with them maintained her language fluency, but didn't build on it.

At this point I asked her why language was a passion for her. It turned out she had been bilingual from an early age (skill set) and had watched hundreds of subtitled films where she saw that the translation was just not in line with the original script. As she described her passion for film translation her eyes lit up and she became very animated (spot the Element). So we built a plan for her to sell her skills as a translator with an ultimate Quest to translate feature films. Her original idea was not far off as it did use her talents and skills, but the environment was not quite right.

Sometimes your first idea is not quite the right fit. Sometimes you only learn through doing that the context for your work needs a bit of a refresh. Sometimes you are just a Square Peg in a Round Hole.

Remember though, that your time Square Pegging is always useful and valuable. Whether you are Maxi at BT, me at the Home Office or Karen teaching kids Spanish, the learning you take with you often proves invaluable somewhere and somehow later on.

Academic Mike Oliver is a disability theorist. He coined the term "social model of disability" to suggest that it is not the disability itself – being in a wheelchair or losing a limb say, that disables a person. Instead, social model theorists believe it is the environment, attitudes, stigma and social structures that disable a person. For example, navigating the Tube in London can be hellish if you are a wheelchair user. The issue is that the environment doesn't support the needs of all the different users. The environment does not provide the support required to enable a person with a different level of mobility to access the service in the same way. Some environments enable us to thrive and some compromise our natural talents and abilities because they do not suit our needs and requirements.

The following exercise is designed to help you take a closer look at the kind of environment that supports you to be your best self.

 Take a real-life example. It doesn't have to be the world of work – it could be a social occasion, a holiday or trip, an education environment, any situation that just didn't work for you. Then we are going to break it down to better understand what it was that made it such a challenge.

- Describe a situation that did not work for you.
- Consider the environment you were in – in what ways did it disable or disempower you?
- What compromises or stories did you tell yourself to justify being where you were?
- Looking back now on the choice you made at that time – what would you have done differently?
- Write out your new statements on the kinds of "round hole" you wish to find yourself in.

The process of self-discovery is not one with an end point. We are changing all the time. Our cells have a "sell by" date of between 15 days and seven years. So in seven years you will literally not be the same person you are now. As we move through our life stages, our priorities change. Experience and wisdom shape our points of view. The world changes around us and different things come into focus.

Now that you've got to the end of this chapter, I want you to make yourself a promise. Promise yourself that wherever you are and whatever you experience, from now on you will use it for your learning, enrichment and growth. Use the nasties, the goodies, the "ahas," the dramas – all of it. Because every experience we have is an opportunity to learn more about who we are and what we are here to do.

 Chapter Summary

- Every one of us has a unique set of abilities, skills intelligence and values.

- The more you focus on what these are, the more confident you can feel and the greater direction you will have.

- There are many methods and tools to uncovering and understanding yourself and your style and these can be really helpful, especially if you have felt or feel misunderstood in your home or work environments.

- Focusing on our strengths makes us masterful; living a heroic life does not mean you have to be good at everything!

YOUR HERO SELF

- What do you now know about who you are and how you function?
- How does this affect the goals you may have set yourself in your life?
- What would need to change so that you could amplify your abilities and use them more of the time?
- What would be your first small step in this direction?
- If you have children, a partner or friends, what could you share from this chapter that could help them discover themselves and feel really proud of who they are?

Fill in the Gaps

What I know now about the kind of hero I am is:

The environment I need to support me expressing more of my passions includes:

Part One

THE CALL

In which we find out what puts the wind
in your sails and the fire in your belly.

3

FINDING YOUR MOTIVE

" I never really wanted to have a regular
9-5 job. What excites me is the
idea of leaving a legacy – producing
something really inspiring and memorable. *"*
Sica Denerly-Weiss, www.reelpeoplefilms.co.uk

So now we understand a bit more about what makes you uniquely you, but to uncover your unique Quest, you need to have a deep understanding of what motivates you. Why do you do what you do? Your type of intelligence and skill set drives what you are good at and how you choose to spend your time. But what gets you out of bed? What is the idea that propels you into your day? If I am here to help you answer the Call and to stay committed to your journey, we need to know what really matters to you, in short, what puts the fire in your belly.

Discovering your motivation is the key to unlocking your Quest. Once you know who you want to be and what you wish to experience, you can begin to find the unique Quest that calls you right now. Furthermore, by the end of this chapter, you will be able to articulate how your driving force, combined with your skills and passion, is setting you up to take action on this Quest.

Heroes always have a sense of purpose around what they are doing. That purpose may have been deliberate and thought out with a long-term game plan. This could be said of Muhammad Yunus, founder of the Grameen Bank, which offers micro-loans to entrepreneurs around the world; or Wangari Maathai, who has enabled millions of trees to be planted across Africa. Motive may occur in an instant, driven by a sense that this is the right thing to do. I remember once intervening to break up a fight in a souk in Morocco. A husband and wife were really viciously attacking one another physically. I had no idea what the fight was about or why other people were walking by, but I needed to help them find a better way to interact with one another. Rosa Parks became renowned throughout history for her civil disobedience in the form of sitting in the "white" section of the bus one afternoon in 1955. Other women had previously performed the same act of courageous disobedience of the segregation laws, but it was Rosa who collaborated with civil rights leaders to lead a legal challenge about the right to sit where she chose. She has since become an iconic representation of someone who stood up for what they believed in. She did it, she says, because she "became tired of giving in."

Your Current Driving Force

Motivations change. They are affected by our health, energy and our stage of life. So it is important to take a fresh look at what you are hungering for today. This is a little different to discovering your purpose in life itself. This is about finding your motivation for this particular scene. A Quest is a project. It may take just weeks or it may evolve over years. Either way, you will need to tap into your deepest level of motivation to find and sustain your commitment to see it through till the end.

II When I started, my motivation was hip-hop itself. The first time I heard it, it was so fresh. You had never heard anything like this in your life. It was something I felt, something I could do. I wanted people to understand how great hip-hop could be. And as I grew as a man and as a musician, I realized there was something even more powerful,

and that was life itself. Your health and your
freedom. To live, transform, shape, mould life from
what it was to what you want it to be. And I
decided I would use those skills to make something
meaningful for me and hopefully, for others. **"**
Maxi Jazz

Sica, who started off this chapter for us, has just made a feature
film for £2000. She achieved this through bringing a large community of filmmakers, actors and key stakeholders across her city
alongside her to share in and enable her vision. Her Quest is to
enter the film into the Cannes Film festival, have it distributed
internationally and win an award for it. A 26-year-old, Bristol-
based filmmaker, she has been working in the film industry since
she got her first break at 16. We will find out more about her and
how she is progressing later in the book.

Why Bother Taking on a Quest?

If life is complicated and busy and challenging right now, why
would we want to respond to a Call? Why put more stress into our
lives and make more demands on ourselves? When our nerves are
shredded, life loses all its rosy glow and you feel like you are at the
end of your tether.

Feeling stressed out or being "distressed" is about the negative side
of stress, the type we seek to avoid as much as possible. The stress
of not having enough time to do something properly or being
pushed or bullied into compromising our principles.

But did you know that stress could also be good for you? Positive
stress, the adrenalin of a challenge, is extremely good for our
mental and physical health. We access it when we take on a goal
that is a stretch for us. This kind of stress is known as "eustress,"
and it is what spurs us on to become champions, to keep going
when we don't know how we will get to our destination. That is

what a Quest is all about – the excitement of the unknown, the adventure and the opportunity to transform. This sense of expansion and learning, even when initiated by the most painful of experiences, enables us to grow.

And this is exciting. Stagnation is a stifling experience. The heroes that most inspire us inherently demonstrate that life is either "a great adventure or nothing at all" as Helen Keller stated. If Helen, born blind and deaf into a quiet and dark world, had accepted the limitations that others perceived her disability to press upon her, she would not have made the inspiring contribution to the world that she did. Helen went on to learn to speak and then to express her thoughts and experiences in ways that touched many people in her lifetime and into the present.

Out of the Ordinary and into the Extraordinary

When a hero accepts the Call, they find themselves entering the magical realm. Things shift out of the ordinary and into the extraordinary. The impulse to try something new begins to beat within us. The desire to reinvent your own story is a very powerful one and once it has arisen, it is hard to shift. The urge to grow becomes compelling. Once we step into our Quest, we discover new aspects of ourselves. We see the world differently. We look different, feel different and act different. We begin to direct focused attention toward one objective. We align others with our mission. Quite simply, a Quest gives life more meaning and fulfillment. It gives us the courage to accomplish extraordinary feats, because we are serving a higher purpose.

Bruce Wayne, aka Batman, became determined to avenge his parents who were murdered by a mugger. He travelled all over the world to study and acquire new skills, including martial arts and criminology. His Batman disguise enabled him to build mystique as he took action against criminals and baddies, including The Joker and The Penguin.

Stand For, Not Against

Before we go on to explore motivation, I want to help crystallize something that is crucial for a Quest. The energy and motivation you put behind your goal needs to be directed in favour of something, not against it. This is true even if the motivation is because you are upset, angry or opposed to a decision that has been made.

Let me give you an example. I am quite involved at the moment in the debate and activism concerning fracking – or hydraulic fracturing. The process is designed to release shale gas from deep within the earth's core through fracturing the ground to release the gas that is tightly packed within it. There is considerable debate concerning the dangers of this process and it has been banned in France, Switzerland and Ireland. As I write, there are demonstrations, of which I have been a part, taking place in a small village 24 kilometres from my home. But I stand not for the anti-fracking movement, but for a frack-free future. Do you see the difference?

We are all motivated by emotion. Almost everything we choose to do, consciously or unconsciously, is driven by the desire to avoid pain and move toward pleasure. The desire to avoid pain can manifest itself as fear of failure, anxiety about the environment, stress about having the courage to change, rather than excitement or hope about the possibilities we can create in the future.

Bertrand Russell is a great example of this in action. Born into an aristocratic family, as a pacifist and humanitarian, he used his position in society to influence and lobby on these issues. He was part of the team that began the Campaign for Nuclear Disarmament in the fifties and often spoke about the importance of co-operative approaches to save mankind. In his autobiography, Russell wrote:

"I have lived in the pursuit of a vision, both personal and social. Personal: to care for what is noble, for what is beautiful, for what is gentle; to allow moments of insight to give wisdom at more mundane times. Social: to see in imagination the society that is to be created, where individuals grow freely, and where hate and greed and envy die because there is nothing to nourish them. These things I believe and the world, for all its horrors, has left me unshaken."

All too often we motivate ourselves by focusing on our againstness – our opposition to something. This has the opposite effect that we intend as it energizes the thing or person we oppose. So don't be anti the way your body looks, be pro its future health and wellbeing. Don't be anti the corporate world or the banks, be pro an ethical way of doing business. Get me?

Good.

Taking a position of opposition will not lead to freedom. It ties you up and it makes it more difficult for other people, who might agree with your views in principle, to get behind you.

" Negativity is totally unnatural. It is a psychic pollutant . . . are you polluting the planet or cleaning up the mess? You are responsible for your inner space; nobody else is . . . *"*
Eckhart Tolle, The Power of Now

This is not to say that anger, grief, pain or sorrow are to be avoided or denied. These emotions are as valid as any other and can be channelled into motivation and drive that creates phenomenal results. But these can be for good or for bad. It is really your choice. In *The Politician's Wife*, a British TV political drama, the wife of a British Member of Parliament discovers he is having an affair. She states, "Anger can eat you up. You have to learn how to use it."

Erica Grigg is a US-based entrepreneur. She runs GetLusty, a website dedicated to the positive expression of sexuality. The site gives couples and singles access to a wide range of resources, from naughty stories to advice on sexual issues. Erica was motivated to start the website to celebrate the journey she had travelled as a survivor of sexual violence.

> *" I wanted to bring something positive into the sex industry. Success to me means my recovery from sexual trauma. It is a key part of my story. "*
> *Erica Grigg, GetLusty founder, www.getlusty.com*

You are reading this book because on some level, at this moment, you know you want to grow, improve, change, shift or expand. Or because you have a sense that there is a cause you need to stand up for.

Before we go any further, take a moment to hear your inner dialogue.

- What have you got on your mind right now?
- What are you motivated to stand for?

Capture your thoughts now.

Understanding your motivation is important because organizations, roles and jobs that require a similar motivation are those in which you will feel most naturally at home. That doesn't mean that professions outside of this motivation are not available to you, or that you cannot have a different motivation and still succeed, but the more you can understand about your own motives and those of others, the more you can use it to get the results you want.

Identifying your own motivation can help you to:

- Ask for more of what you want in specific terms.
- Understand why an environment or relationship dynamic just doesn't seem to work for you and take steps to change it (or your perception of it).
- Be more persuasive and powerful in pitch and negotiation discussions.

The Different Kinds of Motive

Lots of great and interesting work has been done on the different characters that live within us. We can call these the Inner Family. Each family member possesses their own character values and motivation theories. In my time working with so many wonderful and different people across the globe, I have noticed that each of us has one or two primary drivers, drawn from key members of your Inner Family; the seven. Let's have a look at them. As we go through, just notice internally which one your body and heart most respond to.

1. The Caregiver – Motivated to Serve

For many of us, in one way or another, we are driven to serve. We want to find a way to be useful, to play our part in the larger story, to make a contribution and to make a difference. This could be through an invention or creation that has longevity, like a useful product, a beautiful poem, humanitarian work of some kind or the enabling of a change in the way society operates, thinks or behaves.

Shakespeare, in his Summer's Day sonnet, speaks of serving his beloved by commemorating him or her in a poem:

> So long as men can breathe, and eyes can see,
> So long lives this, and this gives life to thee.

If your motivation is service, you are seeking a Quest that enables you to apply your talents to a cause that interests you and that you have a passion for. You are looking for a way to help others. Service includes taking a stand as an activist, a champion of new ideas or being a humanitarian. Traditional superheroes tend to embark on Quests that fall into this category as do classic change makers such as Martin Luther King or Erin Brockovich.

2. The Orphan – Motivated to Be Safe and Secure

Safety is a fundamental human need. Without the basics of shelter, food and clean water, life itself is unlikely. So it is natural that we crave the opportunity to create security for ourselves. If your motivation is security, you may be thinking about how to create a more structured life, a stable job, a better day-to-day routine, some form of treatment or a more healing social group, support a calmer, more structured way of living. You seek a Quest that moves you away from risk and risky environments. People recovering from addiction, retraining or returning to work may often be motivated by this category.

3. The Lover – Motivated to Belong and to Be Loved

Every one of us needs to be loved. Observation of orphans during World War II revealed that a lack of loving touch and contact can be as threatening to the lives of newborns as infection or dehydration. At some stages in our lives, it becomes a strong motivation for us to find places and people with whom we feel accepted and loved. If this is currently an important motive for you, your Quest is likely to be exploring new communities, faiths, or tribes. You may be looking to move home. You may be looking for a new partner or trying to deepen a connection with an existing one. You may be Questing to explore what it is to accept love and receive support.

4. The Warrior – Motivated to Master or Conquer Something

The warrior goes into battle with his own limitations and seeks to master them. Mastery is all about that – the ability to play a tune you could not before, to produce something using your hands that you did not know you could make or the graceful execution of a physical skill such as sport or dance. That's not to say that mastery cannot be cerebral – being free from smoking, getting good at chess and launching a cause or business all fall into this category of

Quest. This is a great area to start your Questing process with and to observe your Hero's Journey as a new skill or talent that is fun to grow, is manageable and that the evidence/results are often really easy to measure.

5. The Creator – Motivated to Produce Something New

If you are currently interested in creating or inventing something new, your motivation falls into this category. This could range from setting up a choir and writing songs for them to sing; designing a solution to a problem, launching a local ale festival, or improving on a product or system that currently doesn't work. Sarah Watkins, one of my coachees, is currently expanding ParentSkool, her peer-to-peer education programme for new parents. This course has been designed by parents for parents. Her drive was to answer all the niggles and questions that first timers have and to help them feel prepared and confident for birth. Her experience with the UK's leading charity, who are the market leaders in providing this education, convinced her more could be done (see www.parentskool.com.)

6. The Ruler – Motivated Towards Status and Recognition

We all want to be acknowledged and appreciated for our efforts and achievements. There's a great episode of the Simpsons where Lisa, the high-achieving and high-functioning member of the Simpson family, gets hyper-anxious wandering around playing tunes on her saxophone and begging for approval, "Grade me!", because no one will give her a grade or a certificate to recognize the effort she has put into a stellar performance. Some of us may really dream of winning a prize or being honoured in some way for who we are and what we have done. But even on a more modest scale, you may be motivated by the fact that you are deserving of recognition that has yet to be forthcoming and this may inspire you to explore different relationships and jobs that offer a more fulfilling dynamic.

7. The Innocent Child – Motivated to Feel Free and Joyful

Sometimes the itch that needs scratching concerns our ability to move, express ourselves and have fun. Your motivation for this area may be high if it has been all work and no play for some time. Perhaps you have had to take on a lot of extra responsibilities or have had to play a role that has required you to be serious, conformist and fairly rigid. We all need time to play and be adventurous. The gap-year student, the burnt-out executive and the person staring into space on the escalator next to you may have just realized that their Calling in life is to be a clown/standup comedian/mime artist etc., and fall into this category.

 Review these motivations. One or two of these are going to be making your heart sing. Don't be shy. Capture it here. Which one speaks most closely to you today? Don't censor yourself. No one is looking. Take some time to articulate what is really motivating your desire for change, here.

More information about heroic motivation can be found in *The Hero Within* by Carol Pearson. For the most comprehensive list of the different aspects that may be present in your Inner Family, seek out the work of Caroline Myss.

Owning Your Legacy

In the film, *A Christmas Carol*, there is this wonderful bittersweet scene where Scrooge finds the whole town in celebration. He joins in the parade, dancing through the streets singing "Thank you very much, that's the nicest thing that someone's ever done for me . . ." only to find that it's his death that is the cause of so much celebration!

When we look at our lives from the perspective of legacy, we are able to take a longer view that can give us courage to begin. Each member of the Inner Family will offer a view about how they want to be remembered. This exercise can help to crystallize for you where your motivation for your upcoming Quest is coming from.

 Imagine you were hovering over your own funeral. Your family and friends are there, all your colleagues and people you have touched throughout your life.

- What would you most like to hear them say about who you are?
- What would you most like to hear them say about how you lived your life?
- What would you most like to hear them say about what you gave them?

The Cost of Refusing to Change: Enforced Motivation

Life has a way of forcing your hand if you do not choose willingly. Think of some of the situations in your life that catalyzed a big shift in you. How many indications beforehand did you have that the change needed to happen? Imagine these as big red flags fluttering alongside your path. These were indicating that something was not right and you ignored them. Until, BOOM! You had no choice but to change. The nudge toward change can be a gentle feather touch. But it becomes firmer and stronger as the urgency increases. We may find ourselves getting more emotional or overreacting. We may become physically unwell. All these are signs that we need to stop, look and listen. In the Alcoholics Anonymous tradition, this moment is called "hitting rock bottom". Everyone has a different notion of what rock bottom is. For one person, it is drinking stolen booze. For another it is having a crash from driving under the influence. For others, their powerlessness with alcohol has to go so far that they kill someone in a blackout and have no recollection of it. Most of us will hopefully never find ourselves in such desperate positions. But the example serves to illustrate that we can choose an empowered motivation or we can wait for it to be forced upon us. If it is our destiny to move or change, life will find a way of letting us know.

How far have you had to go before you hit rock bottom and made a change?

In 2008, two years after I started my social enterprise, The Life Project, I was close to burnout. I had been working hard, but not smart. I had lots of vision and ideas, but no network (red flag 1) and no money (red flag 2). I was digging a great big hole and exhausting myself in the process. Clients were not beating down my door (red flag 3). I refused to stop or reflect or try a different approach. I believed if I kept working harder somehow it would all work out. My health began to suffer (red flag 4). I couldn't sleep (red flag 5). My back started to give way and would leave me flat out for days at a time.

That summer, I was running a camp for disadvantaged young children for a charity in Sussex when one day I took them swimming. I noticed that there were diving boards at one end of the pool and walked onto one. I waited to be told to get off and as I wasn't, I dived. Unbeknown to me, the pool bottom was adjustable and was at its shallowest – only 120cms deep. As I dived in, I was surprised to feel my fingers scrape the tiles. I hit my head on the bottom of the pool and fractured my neck at the atlas – the top vertebrae that is shaped like a cup to hold your skull. It's the same place in fact where Christopher Reeve fractured his. I was incredibly lucky to walk out of the pool. Gingerly holding my neck, I was taken to hospital where I lay flat on my back for six days while the doctors marvelled that I could still feel my feet.

My survival was a miracle. It occurred to me afterward that the Universe had given me the hardest, biggest whack on the head that I could have had to say: you need to stop, this way of doing things is not working. I knew this before the accident, but had ignored it. Or hadn't seen any options. The whack on my head changed my view forever and I began to approach my work, health and client relation-ships very differently. A new life began for me. A few weeks after the accident, with my wobbly head still healing, I won my first sig-nificant piece of work. The weirdest thing was returning to the pool to take indignant pictures of the lack of "No Diving" signs. I was sure I had been wronged. And you know what, when I got there, there were no less than nine "No Diving" signs around the pool. In my blinkered, red-flag world, I hadn't seen a single one.

This is an example of a red flag story. It occurs when we play victim to the circumstances of our own life instead of telling the truth of what we really know about our situation. It's a great exercise to help you understand that your life and your body are trying to motivate you all the time toward an extraordinary and heroic life.

- Name a situation in your life where you have been forced to make a change.
- Now tell your red flag story. Identify all the red flags leading up to that change.
- What stopped you acting on the need to change before you were forced to?

Finding your questing drive

One way to look at what's driving you to embark on this Quest is to view it from a new angle by writing a future scene. A future scene is a description in the present tense of how your life might pan out. It is a few chapters ahead in your story.

So, identify something you might like to do or that you really need to stop doing. Large or small, the purpose is to grasp the concept demonstrated in the exercise.

My Quest could be . . .

- Now, write two short narratives, describing your life, ten years from now.
  - The first is about, if you take this action and make this change, what life will be like.
  - And the second, if you do nothing at all and keep doing what you have been doing, what life will be like.
- Consider, how you will feel, where you will live, what you will be doing, your state of health, who you will be spending your time with and any other aspects that are important to you. Future 1: If I take the Quest . . .
- Future 2: If I stay the same . . .
  - How do you feel looking at these two different futures?
  - What have you taken away from your reflection?

Ways to Uncover Your Motive and Focus on Your Quest

// Great men are little men expanded; great lives are ordinary lives intensified. *//*
Wilfred Peterson

Perhaps by now you are starting to get a feel for what the purpose of your Quest might be. One way or another, there is a desire to create something new. Your dreams matter. They may not be sensible and they may not be understood by others, but your life is your own, for you to mould it into what you want it to be. When you begin to unfold what matters to you and to have faith in what your inner self is called to express, the right action to take will follow on from that.

I am here to support you in discovering your Quest. You may feel you already know what it is that you want to create. If so, these next sections may help you to crystallize your thinking in this area. And if you have no idea, but just know there is more out there, these exercises will begin to give you a sense of your True North. The direction you need to take to uncover greater fulfilment.

What Experience Am I Looking For?

When we ask ourselves about what kinds of experiences we want to have, we lift ourselves above the array of choices for action we could take and instead focus on how we want to feel. Do you want more autonomy and freedom? Do you prefer to work in short sharp bursts? Do you long to give your love to someone or something that would flourish from it? Do you want to wake up with more energy?

- Write down some of the ways you would like to be more of in the future. I'd like to be more. . . .
- I'd like to spend more time. . . .
- It would be amazing to feel. . . .

II Where the needs of the world and your talents cross, therein lies your vocation. *II*
Aristotle

A Quest is the adventure wherein the life situation we find ourselves in, the opportunity to transform it and our passions and skills, all merge.

From where you are sitting in your life right now, have a go at completing these two sentences and answering the following question:

- What I most need at the moment is . . .
- What the world around me most needs from me at the moment is . . .
- What do I want to Be/Do/Have in life?

Normally when we think about our goals, we think in terms of the symbols of success. We think about the evidence that we have achieved our result. We won the cup, we got divorced, we built a big business, we potty-trained our child.

All of these achievements are fine, but the trouble is that we aim for them in the wrong order. We think if we have the car, the relationship, the happy free life, we will be able to do whatever it is we are motivated by and then we will be happy.

We think life works in the order of Have-Do-Be.

But what if life worked the other round?

What if the order was Be-Do-Have?

> **"** We do not see things as they are.
> We see them as we are. **"**
> *Anaïs Nin*

The classic example of this is the loyal and steady employee. He turns up every day to a job he sort of likes, puts the hours in time and time again, so that when he has enough money (Have), he can go and do all the things he enjoys (Do), and then he will (Be) happy and contented.

If we reverse this example, Steady Eddie decides that he needs to find ways to become more happy and contented with himself and his life right now. He begins to get up earlier, to try a new route to work, to spend more time with his children. He works on his stuff, becoming more mindful and aware – more present in his day-to-day work. He notices that a new cycling club has sprung up locally, takes the plunge and joins. Suddenly he has a new peer group, a new hobby to share with his son and a whole new sense of vitality.

When you start from how you want to be, it gives you a whole lot more material to play with. It is my belief that knowing what we want to experience and choosing to act on it is the most healing and empowering thing we can ever do.

Now we know what drives you, we can begin to look at ways to uncover your Quest. Let's tune in and hear the Call.

 Chapter Summary

- Motivation arises through you "standing for" something and having the courage to move towards it.

- You can be motivated either by moving toward pleasure or away from pain.

- Your Inner Family can provoke you to express different aspects of yourself and lead to a surprising Quest.

- Sometimes a powerful motivator can be to look at the impact of doing nothing.

- Start with what you most want to experience, then you can begin to explore what Quest might get you there.

4

HEARING THE CALL

II There is no greater gift you can
give or receive than to honor your
Calling. It's why you were born. And
how you become most truly alive. *II*
Oprah Winfrey

What Am I Here to Do?

Imagine the world as an enormous classroom and life as your personal and tailored curriculum. I believe that we all have a personalized curriculum to follow. Our experiences change and shape us. They help us decide who we are. Life guides us to those unique experiences. They may be momentary one-offs, quantum leaps or patterns that keep coming round for resolution. A Call is an indication that there is a new subject to be explored in your curriculum. A Call always pulls you in the direction of your own expansion.

"We are not in Kansas now Toto."

In the Wizard of Oz, Dorothy finds herself and her house transported to a new world. She discovers that to have a chance to return home, she will need to find and speak to the Wizard. Life has made a choice about a new adventure that she must have and the only way forward is to follow the Yellow Brick Road of her destiny.

This chapter will help you find what is Calling you, to hear it more clearly and turn it into a Heroic Quest.

What do you long to do but fear to give voice to?

We write the story of our lives. Sometimes we are jogging along contentedly, everything seems to be running smoothly and we are enjoying who we are and where we are at. But we rarely stay contented. We begin to feel that something is missing or that there is something more out there for us. We begin to be aware that there are different choices and different lives running along just outside of our line of sight.

The movie *Sliding Doors* is a great example of this. We see Helen (played by Gwyneth Paltrow), go down two completely different paths in her life. These paths are determined by whether or not she catches a particular train at the start of the film. Over the course of the film, we are shown two stories in parallel, each detailing how her life pans out in each of the two paths.

When the Call comes, we begin to realize that some of the stories we have been telling ourselves about who we are and what we can and cannot do, are just that. Stories. Works of fiction. And that therefore, they can be altered. This awareness of new possibilities is the feeling of the Call. The Call is our motive, our reason for making a change or shift that can be large or small, but its impact is always profound.

The Inner Nudge

You know this voice. It may not have spoken to you about your direction or your habits, or it may have done. You will almost certainly be familiar with it from having had a hunch to take an umbrella out with you on a sunny day or not to take a route down a particular street at night. This is the still small voice of your inner knowing. It is this voice/sense that enables you to tune in to your Calling.

> **"** Every blade of grass has an angel over it whispering, grow, grow! **"**
> *Talmud*

When our Call comes, we do not hear it with the ears or the rational mind. It hits us much lower down, within the body. It is a visceral experience. And it is frequently accompanied by the voice.

Once, when I was travelling in Spain, I met a couple of Canadian brothers and we started hanging out together. They told me that their uncle was a historian. He had spent the last 20 years travelling around Europe with his wife in a camper van giving lectures and tours. When he arrived in Berlin or Venice or Montenegro, he emailed his "fan club" and let them know where he was, inviting them to join him on his tour.

When I heard this story, I experienced a shot of internal joy. The hairs rose on the back of my neck. I couldn't stop smiling. I was so inspired by this man's free and adventurous life. I was really happy to learn that it was possible to live such a life of liberty, whilst sharing what you knew and bringing pleasure to others. That was a powerful Call for me. "One day," said my internal voice, "I am going to do that. I am going to take what I know and put my home on my back and hit the road to share it."

 Have you had a comparable experience? Where did it come from?

How to Notice the Nudge

Because the still small voice that accompanies an inner nudge is largely drowned out by our bolshy ego or our inner critic, we need to learn to train ourselves to hear and notice it. Any space you can visit that clears the mind helps too, for example being in nature, in a park, in the woods, by the water. Even if it means taking a short walk round the block while everyone eats their lunch glued to their desk. Your Questing nature deserves a little undivided attention.

Here are three practical tools to support you in hearing the Call and tuning in.

1. What is Making You Curious?

I used to have a very playful boyfriend. He knew it was always a dream for me to write a book and so he used to ask me this question all the time and any time I expressed an interest in something: "Does it make you curious? Do you want to write a book about it?"

He'll be very pleased that his persistence paid off in the end!

The point is, it is a good question. A Call comes from curiosity. Questions you ask about yourself and the world can provide a strong indicator of a Call. Look at your recent internet history. What questions have you asked recently? Take time to listen to the internal dialogue of your Inner Family . . .

Why can't I stop doing . . . ?
What would life be like if . . . ?
How cool it would be to . . .
I really, really must . . .

For the next month, keep a list of everything that interests and inspires you. Whether you hear it on the radio, see it in a magazine or on TV, or an idea just comes to you in a daydream. Track it and log it. At the end of the month, review it for patterns – what is calling you to action?

2. Clear the Clutter

Do what Julia Cameron, writer and creativity teacher, calls Morning Pages. Track your subconscious and its ideas by writing three pages of freeform A4 prose every morning as soon as you wake up. This process helps to dislodge any blocks, fears or other debris that stand between you and your Call. It is also a great place for ideas and next steps to emerge. Don't censor, no one sees these but yourself and they are not art. They are to create space for your ideas to flow through.

Look back over the key influences in your life. What is your favourite album, film or book? Why do you love it? What is it that it calls you to express? Who is your favourite thinker? What is it that inspires you about them?

3. Connect

Spend just five minutes, every day, with your eyes closed. As you close your eyes, start to draw your attention away from your busy mind and further down, through your throat and into your body. Inside your body, regardless of how loud the outer world or in your head might be, the inner body is always still and quiet. Take time to notice how quiet it is. And then, in the quiet, ask yourself, what is my Quest? What is it that I really must begin to do?

Write your answers down.

I've just returned from my fourth year at the Shambala Festival. It's a meticulously well-organized, joyful, safe and happy place to be. This year they even managed to eliminate all plastic cups and bottles from a site containing 11,000 guests and 2000 staff.

Here's what the Shambala team (www.shambalafestival.org) say about their Call.

"We wanted to make a place to party, free our minds, lose our hearts, learn, discuss and be inspired and see what is achievable as a genuine community."

Hearing the Call means staying open to possibilities that you may have discounted before. When I was going mad at the Home Office, I remember sitting at my computer wondering how on earth I would make it through the next few days, weeks, years. And the still small voice said "go running." Now, I knew for sure that this was not me speaking, because I used to hate running. I used to actively mock the futility of taking yourself round in a circle, quickly. It just seemed ridiculous. But then . . . so I bought myself some running shoes, roped in a friend and began to run, in circles round St James Park, which kept me sane until I got the opportunity to leave.

The Three Different Kinds of Call

 Before I give you my version of the Call, let's see if you can work out what is currently calling you:

- What have you been avoiding?
- What have you been dreaming of?
- What would make a huge difference to your life if you changed or reached for it?
- What is going to be a huge hazard if you do not take steps to address it?

The Call: The Beginning of the Hero's Journey

The Call – the impetus to change is different for every hero as every character and every circumstance is unique. Yet, there are actually only three main types of Call out there. Once we understand each type, we can start to notice their influence on our lives.

The three types of Call are:

1. The Roundabout-Style Call
2. The Opportunity Knocks Call
3. The Major Wake-Up Call

1. The Roundabout-Style Call

Some Calls are like a broken record.

Some Calls will keep coming round until they achieve resolution. If you are someone who often gets into disagreements with people or consistently feels cheated, undermined or some other victimized response to life, then it is likely that opportunities to transform this experience will just keep on arising. We see a great example of this in the classic film *Groundhog Day* where weatherman Phil Connors just keeps on living the same day over and over again until he reviews the way he is living his life and transforms his world by taking the right action.

Examples of the Roundabout-Style Call include:

- Continually getting fired.
- Continually getting ill.
- Playing out the same patterns in relationships.
- Getting slightly freaked out by the number of times a course, activity, person, location turns up in your social life and in the media.
- Huge amounts of your energy and time are spent resisting an aspect of yourself or your behaviour that you just cannot stand or feel deeply ashamed of.
- There is something you have always wanted to try and when you mention it to people they immediately say "I could really see you doing that!"

2. The Opportunity Knocks Call

These are the rather unusual and unexpected moments when something falls into your lap. You may not have done anything to encourage it to arrive, but a life changing opportunity has just descended upon you. Here we are, at a busy airport in the mid-nineties. A glamorous lady in sunglasses stops a gangly girl hanging out with friends outside a clothes store. They exchange some words and the teenager takes her card and Kate Moss, the supermodel, begins her career.

Examples of the Opportunity Knocks Call include:

- Being offered a life changing work opportunity.
- Being invited somewhere unusual.
- Receiving an unusual bequest.
- Being invited on a significant outdoors adventure.
- Being contacted by a blast from the past.
- Something you have been waiting for arriving at your feet, all of a sudden.
- Unexpectedly becoming a parent or foster parent.

Opportunity Knocks Calls demonstrate that the Universe has a sense of humour. The unexpected, after all, keeps life interesting. Examples of Quests following this kind of Call include: taking your life in a new direction, going travelling, taking on a significant financial or physical challenge, the steep slope of entering a whole new world of work.

Tim "Mac" Macartney is a leadership expert and the founder of the Embercombe holistic centre. He used to be a gardener. One day he was in the grounds of a leadership institute when two bigwigs came out yelling at each other. He interceded in his peaceful, gardening way and brought their argument to a successful resolution. They were very surprised to discover he was not a professional mediator. Long story short, they invited him to work with them and so his career as a leadership guru began. His story took an even more extraordinary turn some years later when one of his clients asked him what his dream was. He told them it was to design a beautiful nature-based learning space. The man immediately wrote him a cheque. In due course, after much hard work,

Embercombe was born and now offers a wonderful programme of natural leadership and restoration (see www.embercombe.co.uk.)

3. The Major Wake-Up Call

The Major Wake-Up Call is like a firm slap around the chops. These Calls happen to sharpen us up to what is going on around us and once things are seen for what they are, they cannot be undone. They may also require us to hit rock bottom before we notice them. So awareness in this kind of Call can be very painful. Some of these Calls feel very much out of our control and are the hardest things to accept. A sudden bereavement, the loss of a child, an attack or serious injury, these leave us with no choice. The world has been fundamentally shaken and it cannot be undone. Like BC and AD in the Gregorian calendar. There was a life before and now there is a different life after.

In 1998 film, *The Truman Show*, Jim Carrey's character, Truman Burbank, discovers that his whole life has been filmed, staged and set up. Nothing about his environment is real, it all takes place on set and all his friends and family are just actors. This precipitates a breakdown and fundamental questioning of his existence.

Examples of real Major Wake-Up Calls include:

- Becoming aware of infidelity or some other abuse of trust within your environment.
- The news that someone you care for is dying or has died.
- A diagnosis of ill health or a health scare.
- Accidents, injuries or arrest as a result of addiction.
- Awareness that you need to respond to something of local, national, global importance in a pro-active way.
- Being overlooked for promotion.

The Wake-Up Call is a realization that the clock is ticking, that if you do not take action on your own behalf, it will be too late. Wake-Up Calls are designed to avoid regret later in life. Typically, the Quest following a Wake-Up Call would involve a decision to radically change the way you live, how or where you work, or your approach to life.

Prompting Your Call

In your own life, you may be quite clear about which of these Calls are occurring. If not, you may be in a state of waiting or readiness for a Call. To avoid getting stuck there are a few practical things you can do to support yourself.

1. Do Something Different

Do something you have not done before that may unlock a different way of thinking of an undiscovered skill/passion. Learn to juggle, volunteer on a building site, walk to work instead of taking the Tube. Just introduce, every day, a little bit of freshness.

2. Back to Your Youth

- Lie or sit down somewhere comfortable and quiet and relax.
- Close your eyes.
- Imagine as you breathe out that you are bringing your attention and focus into your body, into your rib cage and your limbs. Consciously breathe into your body (rather than your head).
- As you relax, see yourself when you were small. See that child you were, face to face, and ask the question: "What do you want to do when you grow up? Who do you want to be?"
- When you hear your small self reply, check in with your emotions, how closely have you followed that young person's dreams and ambitions? What de-railed you? Are you willing to start?

3. Ask Your Trusted Advisers

Do some research with the people you know and love. They may offer you inspiration and guidance. They may see things that you do not. Check in with them about whether there is an area of your life that you frequently identify as needing action. Or that you are in denial about what is costing you deeply. We don't know what we don't know and sometimes it is only those around us who care and who have the courage to speak out on behalf of our Quest.

At What Point Does a Call Become a Quest?

My Call to write a book tipped the completion of a Quest, which resulted in the book you hold in your hands. However, it is a Quest that began about 12 years ago with the idea that I might be able to use my writing in a way that inspired other people. I have yet to do my European "house on my back" tour, but can feel it coming up in the next year or two. What I have done though, is a number of smaller practice runs, including workshops and talks in Bulgaria, Kosovo, the USA, New Zealand and India to name a few places.

The point here is that there can be a lull or a gap between hearing the Call and starting a Quest. Occasionally, there will be times when your response needs to be almost immediate. Normally however, there is a settling in between the realization of the Call as a reality in your life and the readiness to take action on a Quest. We will explore the question of timing in the Commitment section and explore how best to move through any fear or resistance we need to tackle to move into Questing mode.

In the Marvel Comics, Batman had an early sidekick called Batgirl. Barbara Gordon, as she was known in her "civilian" identity, got shot by The Joker leaving her paralyzed from the waist down. This powerful Call took some time to adjust to. Over a period of months, Batgirl transformed herself into Oracle – a paraplegic hacker and information expert, who provides intelligence and computer hacking services to the other Marvel Superheroes.

Too Many Calls?

You may feel that you suffer from being too inspired, wanting to go in too many directions. This can leave us paralyzed by analysis and anxiety. It can also result in us frittering away our energy by being busy, but not focused and productive. If you know that you are one of those people, know that your great capacity for finding new ideas and possibilities is a talent in itself. To train it, start capturing all your potential Quests in an ideas book. Then look at what you want to be, what you wish to experience. Which of these Calls, at this time, would most support you in creating the experience you want? If you are not sure, take some time out to research and investigate each option. That way, you do not have to say no to something, just to say not right now. The same way that a delicious meal is the perfect thing when you are hungry, but is best deferred if you are full, as you won't truly enjoy it. Prioritize. Go with your greatest hunger. Find where you can make the largest impact.

Jacqueline Novogratz is the founder of Acumen Fund, a venture capitalist organization that invests in ideas that enable development and social change. In her book, *The Blue Sweater*, she emphasizes the importance of deciding on the level of market need for an idea. She tells the story of their investment in a drip irrigation system, which offered a very cost effective and efficient way to get drinking water to local locations and enabled most farmers to double their yields. The organization they invested in, International Development Enterprises (India), headed up by Amitabha Sadangi, sold 275,000 of these systems in four years.

Defining Your Quest

- Real Quests challenge you to be more of who you are.
- Real Quests encourage you to be a force for good or for positive action.
- Real Quests make use of your skills and talents – as identified in Chapter 2.

- Real Quests do not go away, they magnify or become more true over time.
- Real Quests make your heart swell. They may be painful or challenging or plain old scary, but they are motivated more by the force of the heart than the mind.

Here's how Professor Elemental (www.professorelemental.com), alternative hip-hop artist, performer and host, describes the Quest he has accepted:

> "The Professor is the vehicle to do the things I love – so if I want to be in a comic, write a book or a play, I can use him to help make that happen. More than anything, I was motivated by the desire to have fun, be creative and support my family."

Now you are ready to begin defining your Quest, the response to your Call. The choice point comes when you know what you are looking at from every perspective and decide to commit to taking the leap of faith. Having identified an inescapable Call and a Quest we need to decide whether we are committed and explore what is feasible. Let's look at the tools for making a commitment.

 ## Chapter Summary

- To tune into our inner knowing takes time and practice; intuition is your antennae for the Call.
- The Call is the impetus that drives us to start a Quest.
- The Call can be a push or a pull – it can be something we choose or something that is imposed on us.
- It is natural to have some resistance to the Call as it involves change and challenge.
- Timing is important. You may need to allow for some space between identifying the Call and acting on it.

YOUR CALL

My Quest definition:

- What is my Call?

- What experience am I looking for?

- What is my Quest?

Part Two

THE COMMITMENT

In which we say goodbye to the habits and behaviours
that did us no favours and take our leap of faith.

5

LETTING GO OF THE CERTAIN

II We must be willing to let go of
the life we've planned, so as to
have the life that is waiting for us. *II*
Joseph Campbell

Whether our Call chooses us, or we choose it, at some point, we have to take a leap into the unknown. If we keep one foot on the shore and one on the boat, we will eventually fall into the sea, break in two, or rip our trousers. To avoid this unfortunate turn of events, there comes a point where we need to decide to move forward onto the path of the Quest. The trouble is, once you commit, there is no going back and there is also no guarantee of success. Commitment requires letting go of the familiar, the known, and stepping into the new, the unfolding, the unknown.

Tilicho Lake

In this high place
it is as simple as this,
leave everything you know behind.
Step toward the cold surface,
say the old prayer of rough love
and open both arms.

Those who come with empty hands
will stare into the lake astonished,
there, in the cold light
reflecting pure snow
the true shape of your own face.

David Whyte, "Tilicho Lake", *Where Many Rivers Meet*, 1990
Printed with permission from Many Rivers Press,
www.davidwhyte.com, © *Many Rivers Press, Langley, Washington*

In this chapter, we will reflect on how we can see our past experiences as the path leading up to our Quest. We will learn to look with fresh eyes at our lives and at this point of choice. I will help you push through fear, anxiety and doubt and we will work through some of the resistance to change that presents itself in the gap between the Call and the commitment to action.

Out With the Old, In With the New

Like a snake shedding its skin, we need to release what we have outgrown. Some of this decluttering will be easy. It will feel like a release and a relief. However, there will also be things that we are really attached to, that will feel much harder to walk away from or change. When you are thinking about committing to a Quest, you may not even be sure about what you will replace these outmoded aspects of your life with. That's pretty scary stuff. To be heroic, we have to let go of what we have and trust that we will be able to find something better.

First, Learn to See

In order to let go of what no longer works, we have to begin by taking a good hard look at what is. Imagine you have a secret garden inside you. The garden has been forgotten or neglected for some years. Within it there are beautiful and rare plants that have been choked by ivy and fast-growing weeds. Your job is to find these blooms and create space for them to flourish. You decide to observe the garden and notice which parts of your garden get the most sun at which times of the day. You will discover the suntraps and decide where the bench sits. You will notice the animals, birds and insects that call this garden home.

When you discover your Quest, you commit to nurturing your own inner garden so that the best parts of it flourish and you clear out the brambles and ivy that choke its growth.

 Close your eyes. Conjure up your inner garden.
- What does it look and feel like?
- Where does it start and finish?
- What wildlife and nature live there?
- How do you feel about it?

This garden is a metaphor for your inner and outer life. Questing starts with taking this inventory, looking through the lens of the Call at what currently exists in your life. You may find that you see things afresh because you are now looking at them with a view as to how they fit into the future you want to create. Plenty of your skills, experiences and behaviours will be precious and invaluable for this future you want to create, and some will need pruning or review.

For example, let's say you have identified a Quest to change the way you treat your body. Looking around your physical environment you might notice that what you are eating does not nourish your body. You realize you are not even sure what amounts of types of food are right for your body. You may notice that you are not set up with the equipment you need to begin to nourish yourself differently. You might review your routines, such as how much time you spend in front of the telly. You might notice how much you isolate yourself from others, or how your confidence about your body has affected your relationships and leisure activity. You might take an inventory of how much money you have been spending on food and activities that do not support you in the Quest. And you also notice that you have a strong body – a body that moves and sees and responds. You have a big heart that is committed to change. You have smarts – you can find out what you do not know. And you have people who care about you – offering good support to make the transition. Your habits and choices up to now have given you the results you see in your life. If you are to achieve a different result, some of these behaviours will need to change.

II We begin to realize how limited and self-destructive our lives have been, how many opportunities we have missed because of our addictions or attachments, how many people we have hurt or ignored, how much money we have spent. We count the years and months of wasted, unproductive time . . . *II*
Christina Grof, The Thirst for Wholeness

This inventory brings awareness and focus to what is and helps you to start thinking about how to set up a different reality to get a different result. But the first stage, is just to take a good look.

Aspects to observe and consider include:

- The structure of your day or week.
- The choices you make about how and where you spend your time.
- Who you spend it with.
- What your daily environment looks like.
- How you spend your money.
- The quality of your relationships.
- How much of your gifts, skills and motives are given expression in your life right now.

- Looking at your life as it is right now, what can you already see will need to change in your physical world?
- Are you ready and willing to give up or change these aspects of your life to have more of what you want in life?

Inside and Out

" The stories we usually tell only ourselves, make up our self image. Stories about what we are good at and what our limitations are. We can have a story about what our life is about, what we want to achieve, what is most important to us and we can direct our lives to living out this script. *"*
Tony Wilkinson, The Lost Art of Being Happy

Alongside a review of our external environment and circumstances, we need to take an inventory of our internal "set-up." This includes the beliefs we hold about ourselves, what we can do and who we are.

We need to be mindful about the stories we tell ourselves. Why? Because our stories create the world we see. Your commitment to your Quest can only come about when you believe that another life is possible for you. You may have been telling yourself tales about who you are and what you can do that are unhelpful and not necessarily true. The Quest may enable you to tell a new story, from a fresh and more positive point of view.

In the children's story, *The Ugly Duckling*, a little bird grows up feeling rejected and unlovable because he doesn't look like the other little ducklings. He carries this story about with himself and becomes very lonely, isolated and sad until one day, he looks in the water and discovers that he has grown into a beautiful swan. He didn't look like a duckling because he wasn't one.

 What's the misunderstanding that you have been carrying around about who you really are?

Each Quest is a journey in self discovery – in surrendering what we think we know about ourselves and the world.

The fact is, your history need not limit your future. You can commit to the possibility of a different, expanded, more exciting or fulfilling life. You can even use the adversity and challenge of your past as a powerful fuel for your Quest. Heroic characters frequently come from a troubled or abandoned background. They turn this pain into focus and determination that enables them to escape their past, to move toward something better.

Your history does not stop you being able to create a new future. It is up to you to decide who you want to become.

In the film *Good Will Hunting*, we see Will overcome his history and the limitations that others place on him. As a maths genius growing up in the rough streets of South Boston, he experiences abuse and is frequently in trouble with the law. A transformative experience with Sean, his counsellor, helps him to develop acceptance of his past and realize his possibilities for the future. His best friend Chuckie tells him that he is wasting his talent and needs to take charge of his life. Having released his self-sabotage, Will decides to stop being a victim and chooses to leap into an unpredictable but happier future in California with the woman he loves and a deeper recognition of his own talents and gifts.

Like Will, we are going to need to review, recognize and let go of our self-limiting stories and seize the day. When we commit to the Call, we begin to transform our inner world and use any suffering and injustice of the past to fuel our fire. It may take us a long time and a lot of investment to move toward the realization of our Quest. The more we move away from our old story, the closer we get to our new one, until one day, magically, we find ourselves there.

Name a part of your history that you feel angry, resentful or ashamed of.

- What where the facts of what happened?
- What was your interpretation about what that situation meant about you?
- How did that make you feel?
- What conclusions did you draw about the world?
- How much, on a scale of 1-10 with 1 being "not at all" and 10 being "totally," do you still hold those opinions about yourself and your world?
- How useful are they?

"Uncertainty Now Certain"

This 2010 election headline is very fitting to this section. Before you commit to your Quest, you are likely to feel nervous and anxious about the future. Although you may not like where you currently find yourself, you are likely to have a measure of attachment to it. We like the familiar. We can learn to feel at home in the most uncomfortable of circumstances. Even though we are excited about something new and better coming into our lives, we can often panic about the unknown elements of it.

This anxiety is entirely normal. We project out into the future and imagine all sorts of horrors. Or we cannot picture the future at all and feel overwhelmed by how unfamiliar the next chapter will be. This feeling is a sure sign that you are exactly where you need to be to commit – on the threshold – the very edge that we arrive at before we commit. Trepidation is a natural and normal response.

- What anxieties do you currently have about starting your Quest?
- What would help?

A Question of Timing

You may be feeling panicked by the idea of your Quest. Or you may be itching to get started.

Leaving behind what is familiar to you can seem like madness in the cold light of day, for example the financial insecurity of resigning from your job, the pain of ending a close relationship or friendship. How will we live without the comfort of the drugs, the food, the booze? Quests often involve a level of sacrifice and departure before you step through into a new world.

It's important to respect these concerns. Often, when we find our Call, we do not know how we are going to make it a reality. Once the awareness of the need or desire to act comes, you may need to sit with it for a while; allow it to percolate through your system. In fact, it can be quite dangerous to hear a Call and respond immediately without this "settling process." Action taken without due consideration can reduce our confidence in our ability to navigate our journey. So don't be afraid to take time and to let it take the time it takes.

Max Fraser had always dreamed of being a professional musician in the hip-hop world. His day-to-day existence, working at British Telecom, didn't seem to align with this aspiration. Here he talks about the distance between the Call and committing to the Quest:

"During those three years (between deciding to leave and starting the quest) I put pretty much all my wages into paying off my rent debt. I walked into work. I lived off Kit Kats. I saw it as part of the process for reclaiming my own life. Once you understand that you are in a process you can relax because you know what you will end up with, will be more or better than what you had."

The Guardian of the Threshold

II The most difficult thing is the decision to act, the rest is merely tenacity. The fears are paper tigers. You can do anything you decide to do. You can act to change and control your life; and the procedure, the process is its own reward. *II*
Amelia Earhart, aviator

We resist the Call for all manner of reasons that come down to a fear of change. The Call has awakened new knowledge in us. Just like Eve eating the apple in the garden of Eden, we can no longer go back claiming that ignorance is bliss. But we have not necessarily made the decision that the Call is something we are going to pursue and so we sit in the "meantime." The meantime is where we know what must be done, but are not yet ready to take action to make it happen.

We need substantial amounts of courage and faith to help us to take the first steps and actions that will begin our Quest. Some of us may be surrounded by support and encouragement. Most of us will encounter some resistance. This can come from within – in the form of our inner critic, and without, in the voices of those around us.

Portals into other worlds are usually well guarded. They require passwords, the solving of puzzles. Cerberus, the three-headed hellhound of Greek and Roman mythology, stands guard over the gates of Hell.

You might not have an angry mythical dog in your way, but you will have your own obstacles to overcome before you step over the threshold. Let's look at your strategies for dragon slaying.

Dragon Number 1: The Fear of Failure

We all have a fundamental fear of failure. It could be an anxiety about looking bad or silly in public. Or a worry that we will be "exposed" as a fraud or imposter. Or that we will fall short of our own expectations or those of others.

Certainly, if we never tried anything new, we would be likely to fail less. But who wants to curtail their explorations, adventures and experiences just to be on the safe side?

More often than not, we have more regrets for the things we lacked the courage to try, than for the things we had a go at that didn't quite work out. The most successful people in life have learned to get comfortable with failing fast and frequently, so that they can quickly assess what strategy or approach works best to take them toward their goals. Imagine the lack of entertaining competition we would be without in the world if no one was willing to fail. Every sport has to have people who don't win in order for the game to exist. Murray can't "win" Wimbledon without others "losing." No motor racing, no football, no Olympics, no horse racing, no TV game shows. If we never stepped over, out and beyond our fear of failure, we would never reach the new world we want to inhabit.

Meeting Your Inner Critic

While we logically understand this, the hysterical voice inside our head doesn't. The inner critic is like a monkey on your shoulder.

It's the voice that says that what you are planning is foolish and beyond your reach.

In its attempt to help us stay safe and not be exposed or at risk, it puts limits on what is possible for us and it likes saying: "No." "Can't be done." "Drop it." This is because it hates uncertainty and the unfamiliar.

And it's right to be worried. The leap of faith that is required to start us off on a new path is scary. It doesn't come with a guarantee. All through your Quest there will be barriers and challenges. You will still need to amend and alter your course. And you might get to the end of it and find it is not as great as you had hoped. Gulp.

So first of all, it is worth acknowledging the voice of the fear of failure. Recognize that it has your best interest at heart.

If your commitment to yourself is to go on a journey of discovery, you cannot "fail." You can only go on the journey and have the experience you have. You cannot "fail" for example, to take a trip overseas. You do or you don't do, and then you experience the results.

Imagine your inner critic is a hand puppet. Lift your hand up and look at it. Now animate it. Give it a voice. Have a conversation.

- What kind of sniping things does it have to say about you and your Quest?
- What do you have to say in return?
- Is there anything in what it has to say that could be useful to you?

 ## Dragon Number 2: Fear of Upsetting Others

Uh-oh . . . someone is not going to like this

Most people are moderately approval seeking. We want the people around us to love, accept us and recognize our motivations and desires. So when they begin to push against our Calling, it can take quite a lot of courage to speak up for ourselves or to carry on regardless.

The people around us may not like our choices. They may feel we have wasted our education, or betrayed their trust. They may think we are leaping into the unknown without good reason; that we are running away from our responsibilities; that this is not the way things are done.

When I was working as a careers coach for young adults in India, I met a lot of young people who were really struggling because what their family expected them to be was not what they longed to do with their lives. This is your life. You must claim it. To not do so will lead to resentment, anger, depression and pain. This is one of the initiation trials testing the commitment to your Call. Know that it is normal.

Your Quest is not about right and wrong. It is about your personal perspective and aspirations. It is OK for other people to have a different perspective. Their insight may be valuable, their point of view may be understandable. But it doesn't mean you have to agree with it or become defensive. Nor do you need to attack them for their views.

When you listen to their views, try to remember that they love you and want you to be happy. So as you listen, you may find that this changes what you hear. You do not need to defend yourself.

 The next time someone pushes back on your choice to commit to your Quest, try and really hear what it is that is making them concerned. Work out where they are coming from.

When you reply, you might like to try the following:

- "I really appreciate you caring enough about me and my future to share your thoughts with me."
- "What I got from what you said was . . ." then describe what matters to them or what is on their minds.
- "From my perspective this is really important because . . ."

Ultimately, you have this one life. It's not a rehearsal and it is not a play. You do not have scripted lines or roles. Take Jordan, from Series Nine of *The Apprentice*. For the uninitiated, *The Apprentice* is a reality TV show where aspiring young business people battle it out for the chance to work with the British business magnate, Lord Sugar. In the final you get to meet their families and get to know them as people. Jordan's brother says: "The Poulton family boys, we all go into the services. Military, armed forces, police, navy, *that is what we do*."

Well that is nice for you young Poulton, but one look at Jordan and you can tell he is not the athletic type. His gift is different. In fact he gave the Marines a try, but very quickly established it was not for him. He then went on to excel as a very able entrepreneur. We shine where we shine. We all have our own heroic natures. And there is no one else like us. Anyway, it is quite unusual to have a family that always understands and supports your Quest. I am 35 and my jeweller father and lawyer stepmother still say they don't really get what I do.

" Rarely do members of the same family grow up under the same roof. *"*
Kahlil Gibran

That's OK. We can love each other and embrace the difference.

OK, now you are scaring me

> **" I** have spread my dreams under your feet;
> Tread softly because you tread on my dreams. **"**
> *W.B. Yeats,* He Wishes for the Cloths of Heaven

You need to be responsible about who you tell about your Quest, especially at these early stages where the temptation to stall is high. If you know that someone close to you is likely to clobber your sprouting Quest without good reason, consider keeping it to yourself. The Quest, your vision for a better future, for a larger version of you, is in a delicate phase. Be careful with it.

- What are the thoughts that come to you about why you cannot accept your Calling?
- Whose thoughts are these?
- Are they necessarily true?
- What will the impact be on your life if you refuse your Call to accommodate these voices?
- Are you willing to live with this?

 ## Dragon Number 3: Fear of the Unknown

As human beings we are designed for survival. We are born with a very useful in-built fight, flight or freeze mechanism. This means that in times of stress or panic we release huge amounts of adrenalin and make a quick decision about whether to get our spear out, run away very quickly or freeze and try to become invisible to our foe. This is a healthy survival response and is almost impossible to control as it is governed by instinct and survival mechanisms developed over thousands of years of evolution.

However, as it is fairly unlikely that you have recently encountered a bear in your weekend wander around the shopping centre, I am confident in betting that a lot of the time the fear that stops you isn't about survival. It's much more likely to be about what might happen in the future. We call this:

Future
Events
Appearing
Real

So often, we are stopped by what we think is going to happen if we take an adventurous step. We are afraid we will fail, look stupid, get hurt (emotionally or physically) or lose what we already have.

Sound familiar?

The trouble with these fears is that they only focus on one possible outcome from your action – a bad one. But lots of other outcomes could be true as well.

What Else Could Be True?

If we can train our minds to look beyond the first fear-based possibility we see, we can open ourselves up to creating more of the results we want and less of those we don't. We can use our fears to help us focus on what we need to manage or transform. Fear tells us more about what the outcome needs to look like and what we really care about.

In the book, *Everyday Legends* (2006), Jamie Oliver, now a world-famous British chef, talks about his fears in starting his restaurant, "Fifteen" (www.fifteenfoundation.org.uk). Jamie had a vision to train unemployed young Londoners as chefs. We now know there is a happy ending to this tale, but Jamie didn't when he started. He was a nervous hero in unfamiliar territory, just like us:

"From the outset I had loads of worries. Above all I felt totally vulnerable because I was letting 15 strangers into my life. I was going to see more of them than I would my missus, and they might have turned out to be horrible! I also worried about money, how the public would judge me . . . I knew that this could really break me."

Seven years on the Fifteen restaurant chain and apprenticeship concept has proven very successful and continues to grow.

What actions can you take to reduce the likelihood of your future events taking the turn your fear dictates?

When you find yourself daunted and you notice it is holding you back, here are three top tips:

1. Take a deep breath, look the situation in the face and ask – what is the worst thing that could happen here? Would I survive if it did happen?
2. Consider – what is in it for me? Why did I want to do this? What would it give me that I do not have right now?
3. Keep taking action – what is the small step you can take right now that moves you more toward what you want?

Remember that fear and excitement are very close and similar feelings – could this be a sense of excitement rather than fear?

Learning to Have Faith in Life

You and I, we are control freaks. We want to be in charge. We want to know what is going to happen next and what the outcome will be. We want to be sure of this before we even start. But life does not work this way.

If we trusted life to give us the lessons and experiences we needed, we would be able to relax and let go of resistance. If we believed that everything that had occurred in our lives was designed to help us in some way, perhaps we could trust and relax a little more. To do this, we need to question whether it is really true that we are always in control and in charge; and to begin to wonder whether things we might think of as a problem might actually be a gift for us, if we were to look at them a little differently.

As we make progress towards commitment, we can learn to trust that the answers will begin to show themselves. The next step, the right choice, the first action. These will all become clear if we allow ourselves to have a little faith.

- Can you accept the challenges in your life as though you chose them?
- Would you be willing to accept the challenges that your Quest throws at you?
- What would trust in the process look and feel like for you?

 ## Chapter Summary

- Committing to your Quest means leaving the familiar behind.

- Some things will be easier to let go of than others.

- We need to get really honest about what no longer works for us.

- Observation and review are important prerequisites to commitment.

- We need to pass through the threshold guarded by our own inner critic.

- We may have to battle with the concerns, fears and anxieties of others.

- The more we can learn to trust life, the more we can accept both our past and the unknown future.

6

STEPPING INTO THE NEW

II Life expands or contracts in
proportion to one's courage. *II*
Anaïs Nin

We are now approaching the jumping-off point. The time that
you make a formal commitment to your Quest and begin
down the road. We have identified your heroic profile, found your
motive and identified a Quest that really matters to you. We have
reviewed what you will need to change or let go of to begin the
Quest.

Now we are readying up to cross the threshold. This is the point
of no return.

Indiana Jones stands on the edge of a cliff face. He knows that to
capture the Holy Grail he is required to take a leap of faith. He
looks worried, but heroic. He takes a step out into the thin air. As
his foot descends, a bridge appears. He hurtles across the magical
bridge and on to the next chapter of his Quest.

Starting out on your Quest can feel like stepping out into thin air.
To have the courage to do so, we need to cultivate a Questing
Mindset. A Questing Mindset helps us to change our way of thinking so we are more empowered and confident to take risks, like
Indy in the example above. By changing our thinking, we begin to
have more options for doing things differently. This chapter will
give you the practical tools to commit to your Quest with the
courage and determination you will need to succeed.

Attitude Makes the Difference

Cheesy motivational posters were big when I was young. They usually had lions or sunsets on them and people punching the sky. They said things like "Attitude makes the difference" and "Believe in yourself." Apparently they were designed to motivate and inspire the workforce or the student body. There is now a great website dedicated to anti-motivation posters. They include such catchy slogans as "You can't spell failure without U R A" and "What if the purpose of your life is just to serve as a warning for others?" If you feel you need to create a shrine to shirking or just need a way to lighten the tone, you could do worse than check out www.despair.com.

The reason I mention this is that it is important for us to stay playful during our Quests. Yes, they matter. A lot. We may be striving for something that goes way beyond anything we have ever done before. We may be standing for something that will make a difference to many people. But this does not mean we have to go all po-faced about it. Setting big, scary goals for ourselves can be fun. We could look at it as playing the game of life. The bigger the stakes, the more unlikely the odds, the more we can really engage all our faculties. You wouldn't run out to watch a film that had the dramatic movie trailer declaring:

> On this day, in 2014, Dave decided on a Quest. He was going to go shopping. In the frozen aisle, he was torn between the Fudge Sundae and the Rocky Road. Where will it end? What will he take home? Find out in Dave Goes to Cashsavers. Out now.

Decide now to play big. Decide that whatever your Quest is, you are going to go all out to achieve it. Decide that you are going to have enormous amounts of fun doing it. It might be hard, exhausting or challenging, but you are going to make darned sure it is also joyful.

Marina Pepper is a great example of this. Counsellor turned activist, she gave up on local politics when she discovered that she could not make a lasting difference through the system concerning the issues that really mattered to her. Now an eco-activism coordinator, she finds ways to make light of serious situations.

Marina is a bright spark. Beautiful, gamine and alternately playful and serious, she has a great way of using theatre and play techniques to engage people in direct action on serious issues. Over a recent cup of coffee she shared some of her play tactics with me. They included: organizing sleepovers as an alternative to blockades, including pyjamas and bedtime stories, and coordinating tea parties, with bunting and biscuits outside magistrates' courts as a way to support protestors who had been wrongfully arrested.

Start Before You Are Ready

When you start your Quest, you are unlikely to know exactly how you are going to get from where you are now to where you want to be. This is where seeing the Quest as a game can really help. Consider that you need to be in it to win it and you only need to think about your next move. A game of chess can turn on an instant. To play well, you need to be able to observe and survey the board and then take the best and most "right" move you can come up with.

 If you were to create a games rule book for how you are going to approach your Quest, what would it contain?

The three principles of how I am going to "play" my Quest are:

1.

2.

3.

Break the Rules

> **"** Every act of creation is first
> of all an act of destruction. **"**
> *Pablo Picasso*

Questing means freedom to break your previous set of rules. Embrace it! Give yourself the freedom to experiment. Stepping over the threshold can be considered a once-in-a-lifetime opportunity to seize upon a new way of living.

In his book, *A Whack on the Side of The Head*, Roger von Oech points out that every innovation and discovery came about because someone broke the rules and tried another approach.

"With his trailing codas and double orchestral fugues, Beethoven broke the rules on how a symphony should be composed. With his equating mass and energy as different forms of the same phenomenon, Einstein broke the rules of Newtonian physics."

To create a new way of living or thinking, you are going to need to learn to throw away an old one.

Now that you are deciding to go ahead with your Quest, what are you going to give yourself permission to do that you were not allowed to do before?

Be a Beginner

We can employ the idea of the beginners mind to help us get comfortable with entering the unknown. Beginners have wonderful freedom – a license to experiment and to try things out. They can allow themselves not to be any good at all because they are just starting.

Have you ever watched a small child learning to walk? Or maybe you have a little one of your own? It takes considerable struggle and effort to master the art of walking on two feet. Our muscles need to adjust, we need to find and maintain our centre of gravity and get used to being upright. Our brains are working hard to build the neural pathways so that, with enough practice, we can walk without even giving it a second thought. The same is true for the new ways of being we will adopt on our Quest. We are going to need to exercise new muscles, to learn how they work and build up our practice slowly.

When a toddler takes a topple, we don't shout at them and chastise them for trying to take a risk. Instead we recognize and celebrate their success and encourage them to have another go. In no time at all, they are waddling about all over the place, leaving carnage in their wake. We need to find the ways in which we can celebrate our baby steps as we begin, holding back the inner critic to protect these vulnerable new aspects of ourselves and our emerging Questing skill sets.

Gratitude for Growth

Learning to be grateful for everything that life throws at us, the curve balls, the pain, the surprise, is an important tool in the work of the hero. Even when we are feeling desperate or lost, there are ways to be grateful. And gratitude as a practice helps to open us up to more happiness and faith in the order and rightness of our experience, no matter how challenging.

You may find it helpful to begin a ritual of gratitude. Every day, take some time, perhaps just before sleep, to note and appreciate things about which you can be grateful. Think about your day, your environment, the people you met and the things that happened. Find three or four things that you are genuinely delighted about. Gratitude can act as an antidote to uncertainty and helps to ease the effects of any unhappiness we may have about our current condition.

I remember the first time I tried out a static trapeze. It had always been a dream of mine to wear spangles and go flying above the crowd. I seek out aerial theatre and am always captivated by the beauty and speed of those daring circus performers, graceful and strong and seemingly fearless, as they swing high above my head in the Big Top.

So the first time I had a go, I donned my action-woman leggings, dusted my hands to stop them slipping and placed them on the swinging bar above my head. The teacher told us to gracefully raise both our legs forward off the floor using a little jump for momentum and then lift them over our heads in a "pike" position. I tried that. But my legs were determined not to leave the ground and my arms just shook like jelly. The only part of my body that I could get to go upwards, in defiance of gravity during that session, were my eyes.

But you know, within five weeks, I could not only move into this strange gymnastic position, I could get up on the bar too.

 What are you going to be trying for the first time on this Quest?

Think of yourself as that little toddler, making the epic journey from sofa to table. If you allowed yourself to be a beginner, how would you take care of yourself while you are learning?

Stop Believing in Safety

Seth Godin, social media guru, points out that the idea of staying safe is itself a myth. We think if we do nothing, we will never be exposed. "Selling is not safe. You might (in fact you will) be rejected. Golf is not safe. My grandfather died playing golf."

If you wholeheartedly commit and step out of your place of safety, the worst that can happen is that you learn from your mistakes. If you don't begin, you will never know what could have been.

As an aside, Seth is one of my role models. He doesn't mentor me. I have never met him. I just like his style. Who are your role models? Who are the people who do something a bit like what you would like to do? How can you find out more about them and use them as inspiration for the Quest?

Eliminate Failure as an Option

Until the Quest is done, you have no idea whatsoever about how it is going to turn out. Given that you have no information at all to base this on, you need to keep your mindset focused on the question of "How can I succeed?"

Joss Whedon's TV show, *Buffy the Vampire Slayer*, shows Buffy constantly finding herself battling all manner of demons and bloodsuckers in her Quest to save the world from the dark forces. Whatever challenge she faces, whatever variety of scary monster, she remains confident that, as Armageddon is not an option, she will find a way through, either on her own or with the support of her friends.

When Helen and Simon set up Montezuma's, a family-run luxury chocolate business (www.montezumas.co.uk), they had no idea how it would do. The original plan was only to sell chocolate, but when their manufacturing supplier went bust, they started making the chocolates themselves. Having invested all they had and ignored everyone who said it was a bad idea, they really needed to do whatever they could to make it work. Helen told me that "knowing you could lose everything is a great way to focus the mind and motivate you to do whatever it takes!"

If you knew that failure was not an option on your Quest, what preparations would you make for stepping into the new?

The Courage to Begin

So now we have the mindset in place to really launch our Hero's Journey. Next bit. Hmmm, chew that pencil . . . how do you actually start?

You do not need to know how you are going to do something before you start. The "how" emerges from clarifying the "what" and the "why" and then repeatedly taking action. Thomas Edison, inventor of the light bulb, was absolutely certain that it was possible to use a metal filament to conduct electricity and therefore produce light. He didn't know what metal, at what thickness, but he was absolutely clear about his intention – to create a light that worked. It took several thousand goes to find the right filament, but Thomas's commitment was undimmed (excuse the pun). Edison told himself each time the light did not come on, that he had discovered another way that did not work. Until one day, it did. Stepping into our Questing world requires this level of commitment. If it is not the first or the second or the third solution that works for the result you want, you will just need to keep on coming at it from a different angle.

In order to help you learn to initiate and commit, we are going to look at three tools.

1. Set a date
2. Start small
3. Build new habits

1. Set a Date

Now, not to state the obvious, but a date in the diary does wonders. So give some thought as to when the best time for you to start is and put it in the diary. As no one else will care as much about your Quest as you do, an artificial deadline can help you make a start. Another way to do this is to make an external commitment to someone concerning your Quest. For example, if you are dreaming of going to college, book a place on the open day. The action does not have to be huge, but there does need to be a real and significant activity that takes place to denote the start. Someday, sometime is not a Quest. A Quest is a factual commitment to making something happen. And it has a start date and a tangible action.

2. Start Small

II A legendary hero is usually the founder of something – the founder of a new age, the founder of a new religion, the founder of a new city, the founder of a new way of life. In order to found something new, one has to leave the old and go on a Quest of the seed idea, a germinal idea that will have the potential of bringing forward that new thing. *II*
Joseph Campbell

If your Quest is a challenging endeavour, something that has not been done before or one that will involve significant finance, time or energy, you might want to experiment with a trial run before you commit to it fully. In my workshops, we call this a "pilot." In TV it can prove very costly if a whole series is made that does not capture the interest of viewers. A pilot episode is a one-off, low-budget version of the whole shebang. It tests the concept, the vision and whether the tone of the programme hits the mark with the intended audience. This then gives TV executives a chance to decide on whether to invest a lot more money in the whole series. Before you quit your job and move to Norway to set up an eco tree house resort, plot vengeance on a bullying boss through exposure in the press, join the world's most expensive dating agency or buy an entire suite of woodwind instruments, just consider first of all:

"What is the micro version?"

Ways to Test Out Your Assumptions About What This Quest Will Give You

There are many ways to get a taster for a new career. You could job shadow, volunteer, meet with people who do this new role you are considering. For start ups for example, can you pilot your concept in a small way – if you want to open a retail outlet, you can get a feel for whether your product will be popular through a day at a car boot sale or farmers' market. If you want to write that novel, can you join a class to experiment with the production of a short story? If you are thinking about starting a family, can you borrow some children for the weekend? The scary statistics on business start-up failures (78% fail in the first year) are due in part to this. People decide on a radical change in their lives, they haven't planned it, researched it, understood the implications and they have spent lots of money to get it up and running only to realize it doesn't work or it will work but will take a lot more money or time that they have. Some people take years training in a complex skill set only to discover that they simply don't like it. I have coached a surprising number of junior doctors who have spent eight years in intensive study only to discover that they are not keen on the only profession their education has qualified them for.

Save yourself this kind of bother by test-driving your Quest. With my start-up entrepreneurs, I consider it a real success to run a pilot and discover your idea is not viable. Imagine if you had gone ahead – the stress it would have caused. Like Edison, you have just discovered one other way that does not work. This does not mean the end of your Quest, it means you are one step closer to discovering what will work to give you the experience you are looking for.

And if in doubt, keep returning to what you know about who you are and what you are committed to experiencing in your life.

- What are the ways this could be expressed that differ from your first thought?
- What could you do by way of an experiment?

3. Develop New Habits

I want you to do a little exercise for me. Hold your hands out in front of you, with the palms facing each other. Now clasp your hands together, interlinking your fingers like this.

Notice, which thumb is on top? The one on the left or right hand? Now I want you to unclasp your fingers and do the same thing, only put the other thumb on top. So your left is on top, instead of your right, or vice versa.

How does it feel?
Weird right?

We all have habitual ways of doing things. If you play football, you will know that there is one foot that just feels more comfortable to kick with. The same is true emotionally – there are some situations in life where we can pretty much predict how we are going to behave or react. Think of how you are with a parent or particular friend. Do you act differently based on that relationship? And if you are stressed or upset, do you tend to do the same sorts of things to comfort yourself? I do. For me, it's hiding away in bed with a movie. Now maybe sometimes, the best thing for me to do would be to go for a walk, or to distract myself by seeing someone fun, but it feels uncomfortable and unfamiliar and the quicker, more habitual, fix is to get back into bed.

But here's the thing. "If you keep doing what you've always done, you'll always get what you've always got." Which is fine if your life is totally perfect and you are glowing with health, have great relationships with everyone near and dear to you, value and appreciate yourself, contribute positively to society, have the wittiest and most marvelous friends, speak a range of languages, can reasonably be described as a polymath, have an astonishingly fulfilling job and a clear sense of purpose. If this is you, you may as well put this book down right now.

Still here? Thought so! We all have areas we want to improve, new talents we might like to explore, habits we want to break. Yet sometimes we get a little stuck, because what is familiar feels safe, even if it isn't such a great idea.

Whether it is leaving a job or a marriage, starting a family, changing direction, starting a business, giving up smoking, setting off on a physically demanding adventure, launching a campaign, whatever you dream of, you will need to break some habits and do some unfamiliar things.

If you start with simple habit breaking and get comfortable with this, you can move on to more advanced techniques in due course. Habit breaking is a great way to train yourself to adapt better and more quickly to change.

Do Something Different

You are going to need to make some shifts in your behaviour when you commit to your Quest. We talked in the previous chapter about how to observe and review your environment. As we step into the new, some simple behavioural changes can support you in maintaining your Questing mindset. You will need to find the ways to make time for the Quest sacrosanct and hold yourself accountable.

Positive new habits might take the form of five minutes in the morning, spending time connecting with your Quest. It might be the list of small steps you will take today that you compile over breakfast. You might designate a particular room or desk space in your house as Quest HQ. Perhaps you could download a playlist of inspiring songs and make a commitment to spend five minutes every day dancing to *What a Feeling* or *Don't Stop Me Now* or some other energy-inducing positive song! Find a ritual that works for you that will give you the sense of familiarity and support you need to ensure you regularly connect with your Quest.

To write this book I created a ritual of getting up at six in the morning to write for three hours every day. I would turn up, whether I fancied it or not. If I avoided this ritual, I found I started coming up with all sorts of excuses, reasons and avoidance techniques. These included watching TV programmes I wasn't interested in, eating when I wasn't hungry and reading the newspaper cover to cover. Nothing wrong with them in themselves, but I didn't even enjoy those things because, in the back of my mind, I KNEW what it was that I needed and wanted to be doing. The more I resisted it, the more uncomfortable my life became. Your precious energy is being frittered away on worrying about not doing what you should be doing.

- What are your non-negotiable rituals?
- What can you commit to, even if you do not feel like it?

Kicking the Habit

If you want to change a habit – maybe you eat late at night when you aren't hungry or you want to give up smoking, try interrupting the habit with a new activity. Breaking or changing a habit is achieved through the sustained practice of doing something different. This repetition embeds the neural pathways that change the passage of Emotion-Thought-Action in your head.

If the behaviour you want to stop seems compulsive and it feels like you do not have a choice about it, another way of taking a baby step, is to delay by one minute, whatever it is you plan to do that you'd like not to do. Just wait 60 seconds. This pause enables you to collect your thoughts, feel calmer and, even if you do then take the action, you have already achieved a measure of control. Each time the compulsion hits you, make it a game to pause a little longer. And each time recognize your achievement.

What would be the most useful new habit you could develop to support your Quest?

What action could you take every day to demonstrate your commitment to a new life?

When Commitment Is Forced Upon You

When life "happens" to us, the only choice we are left with is how we respond to it. Once we have begun to move through shock or denial, our head begins to look forward to the future and we may find comfort and focus through our commitment to a Quest.

Remi Olajoyegbe is an entrepreneur, a coach and the co-founder of Six Dinners Later, a face-to-face social network that enables members to make new friends through hosting and attending dinner parties in each other's homes. Remi had been very successful in the financial markets for several years before a painful loss catalyzed her decision to change her life completely. "I already knew that what I was doing was no longer fulfilling me. But when my daughter was still-born very late on in my pregnancy, that was a key decision point. It was deeply traumatic, but I can honestly say that she changed my life and she really highlighted my need to nurture. I felt I needed to channel her loss in a positive way. Shortly after she died I changed direction completely, retrained as a coach and began the entrepreneurial endeavours I had long thought about but not actioned."

If your Quest has been catalyzed by some kind of tragedy or shock, what can you do to transform this energy into positive action?

Taking Your Vow

In 2012, I was fortunate enough to become a Winston Churchill Travel Scholar (www.wcmt.org.uk). This bequest lets any UK citizen apply for a bursary to take a once-in-a-lifetime trip to examine an area of passion or interest and bring back what they have learned to the UK. The key question for the participants is: how will you share what you have learned in a way that benefits UK life? It is not enough to have the experience of the trip – the experience is validated by sharing it with others. This book is part of my giving back what I was so graciously given by the Trust (my area of interest was transformational education).

A vow is a promise we make like the question asked by the Church-ill Trust. It sets out what we will do in the way of dedicated service to the world in exchange for support on our Quest. We need to find a way to give of ourselves in order to achieve something that matters to us. You may have done this at times in your life where it felt necessary to strike a bargain – "If you help me with this I will . . .". Mythology abounds concerning the dark side of this pact – where characters call on dark forces to help them achieve their goals. If we are to stay in the light, the strength we need to call on must be clear, positive and sacred.

> *"* I decided that everyone had their own personal God and that however much faith you placed in your own God, determined how successful you could become. I made an agreement then, with my own personal God, that if he would keep the wolf from my door, if he could allow me to be a professional musician, then I would, for the remainder of my days, use my music to touch other people and to sing his praises. *"*
> *Maxi Jazz, on his commitment to share the principles of Buddhism through the platform of being a successful musician*

Whether you draw strength from a spiritual belief or consider yourself profoundly rational, you may wish to take your own Vow. It could be one of loyalty or commitment to yourself and your mission. Or it could be a promise about what you will bring back to your friends, family or community on your return.

For those of us who do have a spiritual foundation, or who might like to develop one, we can use prayer and silent, quiet time to make our Vow.

- How would you articulate your Vow? What gift are you willing to share with the world as a result of your Quest?
- What might you be willing to sacrifice, surrender or give up in order to have the outcomes you are looking for?

Close to the Edge

" Icarus was warned to fly the middle path, not to fly too close to the sun or the water. When you are doing something that is a brand new adventure, there is always the danger of too much enthusiasm and emotion. We have to learn to keep our mind in control and not let it pull you compulsively toward disaster. *"*
Joseph Campbell, The Power of Myth

Whatever your Quest, there may be preparations to be made before the jumping-off point. I may be asking you to jump out of a plane, but not without a parachute. Sometimes these preparations take time and effort to put into place. We become impatient to get started, tired by the seemingly endless list of components, or qualifying tests or different plates we need to spin.

If you are going to begin an endeavour that will be costly, or will mean you are unlikely to be earning money for a period of time, this will need to be managed. Yes, heroes do often have real luck and serendipity, but you need to both "trust in God and tether your camel." If you are returning to study, setting up a new business, taking time out for a physical adventure or becoming a parent, you are going to need to consider how material needs will be met. This may mean a delay in beginning the Quest, or a rethink of the format of your Quest to allow for some part-time work or the acquisition of savings. It could also be achieved by cutting down your expenses and living more simply.

Financial and security worries can reduce the level of energy we have to focus on the Quest ahead of us. We rarely do our best work in these conditions.

Every Quest involves some level of sacrifice.

- What are you willing to give up to begin your Quest?
- What have you put in place to support you financially?
- What adjustments might you need to make to your life to accommodate your Quest?

Just Do It

The good news is that all evidence points to the release of a lot of positive and energizing effects that result from committing to and beginning a Quest. The montage scene from every classic hero story, where the hero gets fit, gathers weapons, finds mentors, seeks knowledge, falls in love . . . all those experiences mirror what happens when we commit to a life plan that means something to us.

You might like to see this jumping-off point as the entry point into a more magical and alive way of living where we have to rely on intuition, collaboration and resilience to see us through. Though Quests are, by their nature, demanding, this is usually a really exciting time. So be sure to enjoy it.

The Jumping-Off Point

The Universe rewards action. Our heroes, real and imagined, take action on their dreams. They learn through doing. There is a limit to the amount of academic or theoretical research that we can do on a subject. At some point, we are going to need to start. And when we do, we will learn a huge amount from our research in action.

Quests Activate Superpowers

My friend Caroline came to visit me a couple of years ago covered from head to toe in nettle stings and bramble cuts. Just looking at her skin brought tears to my eyes. She had taken her sister's skittish racing horse for a ride and the horse had reared up, thrown her off and bolted. She had fallen hard, onto her back and into a quagmire of nasty plants. But as she fell, her first thought was "I need to catch that bloody horse." The adrenalin kicked in and it was not until the horse was safely recaptured that Caroline registered how hurt she was.

So it is. We are going to need to shoot out of the nettles and long grass and leap over the fence. We are going to need to take the step we do not want to take. We are going to have to let go of what happened moments ago, months ago or years ago, to be present with what is, right now. We are going to run for our lives.

Come to the edge.
We might fall.
Come to the edge.
It's too high!
COME TO THE EDGE!
And they came,
and he pushed,
And they flew.

Christopher Logue, "Come to the Edge", *New Numbers*.
Reproduced with permission of the state of Christopher Logue
© Christopher Logue, 1969

 Chapter Summary

- To step into the new we will need to be willing to break the rules.

- We can take both solemnity and play into the spirit of our Quest.

- If we start small and practical, pilot our ideas and do our research, we can make it easier to begin.

- We can build habits that support who we want to become.

- Take ownership and manage the practicalities.

- Commitment starts with action – at some point we have to be willing to jump.

YOUR COMMITMENT

Time to make your commitment.

- What prevents you from committing to your Quest?

- What can you put in place to remove these obstacles?

- When will you do this?

Name and describe the attitudes or qualities you want to approach your Quest with.

- What is your vow?

- What will you take with you into your future?

- What do you need to leave behind?

Part Three

THE QUEST

In which we gallantly bound into action, make a plan,
build a team and survive the Supreme Ordeal.

7

QUESTING IN ACTION

" I like living. I have sometimes been wildly, despairingly, acutely miserable, racked with sorrow, but through it all I still know quite certainly that just to be alive is a grand thing. *"*
Agatha Christie

Questing after something that you stand for, that you believe in, that you desire to experience, is the ultimate experience of being alive. Your Quest may be dangerous, frightening or tiring, but it will also be educational, inspiring and a journey of deep self-discovery. When we Quest, we become unreasonable – determined to find a way to our destination, no matter what. We know the way will be challenging and frightening, but we are buoyed up by the mysteries of life that come to meet us when we cross the threshold.

Having taken the leap of faith and passed your initiation, the first period of the Quest is often like bursting out of the starting blocks. You are filled with energy and power to move forward, out of nowhere, a "red carpet" of support seems to open up, with people, funds, resources and ideas coming in thick and fast to support you on your new adventure.

Imagine yourself at the bottom of a mountain with the sun on your back and the wind in your hair. As you observe the challenge you have set yourself, you feel the weight of the pack on your back – your preparation, your determination and your willingness to try.

You know that you may not be able to scale this mountain. You know that you may risk your life trying. But here you are. Behind you lies the path that got you to this point. Alongside you are the friends who believe in you. Ahead, the grand adventure. This is where you find yourself. Take it in.

This chapter will help you to identify and plan the steps that will give you the best chance of success on your Hero's Quest. To fulfill your Quest, you will need to learn to break it down into manageable pieces, to track your progress, to become comfortable with changing course and manage the risks involved. When this chapter is done, you will have a plan you can work to that will evolve as you progress, climb and traverse the mountain. So let's take that first step.

What Does Success Look Like?

Before you make a journey plan, you have to choose a destination. You should by now have the headlines in the form of your Quest Mission and your Vow. But what will success look and feel like? It's time to paint your vision of the future into glorious Technicolour. Just as if we were heading to a specific fireside at an idyllic pub in a rural village in Wales, it would not do to open a national map and hope to find the exact co-ordinates, so we need to approach our Quest and the steps to get there with a new level of specificity.

The Quest may not take the exact route that you map out. But without any kind of plan or barometer for success, how can you know if you are heading in the right direction?

In the British Army they like to use the phrase:

"Fail to plan = plan to fail."

Our Questing success depends on a combination of clarity of intent, a structured approach and the support we receive from above, below and within.

Where You Look Is Where You Go

In the 2008 documentary film, *Man on Wire*, we watch Philippe Petit, a young tightrope walker, devise his plan for how to walk between the newly-built World Trade Centre towers. Petit was inspired by the sheer scale of this new building. The Call got stronger and he committed to accomplish this feat. We hear about the process for his training, the strategy devised for guerrilla entry into these high-security buildings and the engineering required to create a sufficiently taut wire for him to walk across.

Success then, in his Quest looked like:

Create a secure tightrope between two of the highest buildings in the world and successfully traverse it more than once, before being forced to come down.

This goal is pretty tangible. You either create a secure tightrope or you don't. You either make it over from one tower to the other or you, errr, don't. You either buy enough time to be able to complete one traverse or you get arrested or rugby tackled. He managed to perform several acrobatic manoeuvres on 7 August 1974 before handing himself over to the Port Authority police.

Now it is your turn.

- What would have happened in your internal or external world if you succeeded in your Quest?
- What tangible evidence or goals would you need to see?

Measure What Matters

> " Not everything that can be measured
> matters, and not everything
> that matters can be measured. "
> *Albert Einstein*

In my work as a consultant I am often asked to help organizations measure how successfully they are serving their customers' needs. Now all credit to them for wanting to quantify their impact. Accurate information of this kind helps them to discover what investments are paying off and better understand why customers love or loathe their brand. So theoretically it helps them to do more of what works. Which is all good.

The only issue is, are they measuring what matters?

Very often, I will find that what is being measured by the company is not the same measure that matters to the customer. For example, many call centres will track how long a call takes and try to reduce the duration of that call, forcing the operator to "close" the call within a certain time. This is of interest to them for two reasons. One, they want their customers dealt with promptly and two, obviously, the less time it takes, the more calls can happen and this means the operator is more productive. Except that most customers would rather have one call that takes longer and have their query or problem resolved the very first time they call. This is known as "first-time resolution" in customer service circles. So there is a lot of data showing how many calls are resolved in less than five minutes and lots of rewards for short calls, but no one is checking how long it takes to get a first-time resolution – which is what the customer actually wants. The more the customer has to call to chase the problem, however short the call is, the more annoyed they get.

What gets measured gets done. So the operatives will terminate the call within five minutes if they can, even if this means the poor caller has to keep calling back to get an answer to their problem.

The same is true for us on the Quest. Is getting something done fast more important than getting it done properly? Sometimes it is. Sometimes the timing is really the most important factor. Other times, getting the right result, with just one shot, would be the priority. So, for example, you might delay your first escapade on your flying machine if you are fairly certain that there is a problem with the propeller.

Eco-activist and coordinator, Marina Pepper, recently coordinated a two-week sit-in at Trafalgar Square, Marina made sure that there were two tangible goals to the event so the organizers could track success. These were: 1. Educate and raise awareness of the climate change issue and 2. Take direct action every day.

We are now going to work out how to measure for the right result. Look at your Quest again. Jot down here what measurement matters most.

What format will you use for this measurement? Is it a number? A weight? A location? Does the experience you have along the way matter? For example, do you want to be gentle in the way you learn? Do you want to feel a sense of excitement? Do you need to feel challenged? How would you assess this?

II Any mission-driven organization has got to have some way of planning their campaign and measuring the success of the things they are trying. There are things we spent a lot of money on that really didn't work for us, that I wish we hadn't done. But I was able to know when to stop them early, because we were tracking the number of new online community members each activity or method brought in. *II*
Erica Grigg, on developing a marketing strategy for her website GetLusty.com

How Do I Know When I Am Done?

There is a great pub in Brighton that offers delicious Reggae Roasts. These are Jamaican Sunday dinners produced from scratch, at Rasta speed, which is a little slower than regular time and produces great results. Anyway, the timing for attending dinner on a Sunday is specified as "one till it done."

Sometimes, our Quest is like that. How will we know when our goose is cooked? Our dragon slain? Our Quest complete? What if the Quest is a life's work? Quests can be this way. Some have very definite endings, for example, running a marathon. Whilst others, continue to evolve and deepen as we move into them – for example devising a new therapy technique or teaching a class.

The important thing is to define some interim or shorter-term goals. We take our best guess and correct as we go along. If your Quest does have a definite end date, marked by an event such as a wedding, then you can set a goal date. Where you get to by that date may or may not be where you expected. Having a date gives focus to time and helps us to decide what will give us the best result within that time bracket. An example of this is the time I ambitiously set myself the goal to write and perform a one-woman show at the Brighton Fringe Festival. Because I am someone who needs external targets to focus on, I signed up early and put my name in the brochure with some blurb about the show. Now I was committed . . . to a show I had not actually written.

As the months drew closer and I threw away draft after draft, I was getting into a real panic. Tickets had been sold. I needed to have something worth the audience's time and effort. One day, one of my theatre friends told me about the idea of a "scratch performance." This is a pilot. A first draft of a show. She said that I would need to see the performance as the first scratch. Good enough to watch but definitely a work in progress. Once I heard this, I felt an immediate sense of relief. It didn't need to be perfect – it could be the best I could manage in the time I had. The show was called

Some Kind of Madness. An appropriate title, given my Questing approach to it!

If you are trying to set a record or to get something done within the quickest time, you may need to compromise or be flexible about what the solution will look like in that time. You may need to be happy with getting to a prototype of something you want to create, or sacrifice in some other way.

Clarity of Purpose

II A painting is never finished – it
simply stops in interesting places. *II*
Paul Gardner

A huge amount of effort can come to nought without a clear goal. This is particularly true if you are rallying a large number of people behind a shared goal. Without clear objectives, the cause and measures for success can easily get lost. The Occupy movement (an international protest movement against social and economic inequality) went this way in 2011. Despite the tremendous movement of support from around the world, the number of goals and objectives for the movement got increasingly diluted until no one knew what the story was or what the protestors wanted.

If we are working toward a cause, the cause itself may go beyond our original Quest and turn into a lifelong vocation. The work of campaigners for justice, like Liberty's Shami Chakrabarti; or for ethics and animal welfare in fashion, like Stella McCartney, can offer examples of this. The Lawrence family are an example of lives that have become defined by the work they do. Their son Stephen was killed outside his school in a racist attack in 1993. Since then, his family have been instrumental in highlighting the existence of institutional racism within the police force and have worked tirelessly to have his killers found and brought to justice.

A life's work is a life's work. Whatever the duration of your Quest, it is important to find ways to mark, track, monitor or celebrate progress.

This can be achieved by breaking down your larger goal into smaller ones.

And that is where a little project management might just come in handy.

Meeting Your First Milestone

Our work so far has been about the bird's eye view. The high-level goal and the broad vision. Understanding who you are and where you are going. This destination is important. It builds motivation and focus. Turning an idea or grand goal into a reality is going to require a plan and a route map. It is going to require putting one foot in front of the other. As we embark upon the Quest, we must now focus on the worm's eye view. The devilish detail. The next step.

Johannes Moeller is the founder of Edventure. Edventure offers a year-long training in how to create a sustainable and ethical business. The "school" has just graduated its first year of students.

" I had a magnificent idea of what Edventure was for and what we would do. When we actually landed in Frome and the dust had settled, I began to realize that this enormous project was going to have to be completed in minute, bite-sized chunks. *"*
Johannes Moeller, Edventure, talking about taking the first steps to plan and realize his vision

I have a postcard above my head that says Do One Thing. When we know we have an enormous challenge to face, we can easily become indecisive, lose energy or focus. This card reminds me to just take the next step in front of me. In time, these add up to the total journey. To help you focus on your Quest, let's take some time to explore the Milestones along the way.

What Is a Milestone?

Milestones can still be seen around the UK. They provide the traveller with a sense of how far they have come and how far they still have to go to reach their destination. Your satnav does the same, tracking down the time and distance between you and your final destination. In the same way, once you have decided to embark on your Quest and left the safety of the shore, you will need some indicators that help you know you are heading in the right direction.

You can do this by defining your own Milestones. Milestones are checkpoints en-route to your Quest. They have tangible goals that you can measure as a way to evaluate your progress.

A Milestone is a significant stake in the ground for your Quest. It is the end of a mini-project of its own.

Let's map out an example.

Say your Quest is to live a peaceful retirement in a restored watermill. That is your ultimate destination.

And right now, you live in Croydon, a town on the outskirts of London and do not own a watermill. This is where you are at the start of the journey.

There are a number of checkpoints that you will need to pass through to get you to your watermill. You can track these through setting Milestones that break down the big goal into more manageable chunks.

So the Milestones you might set yourself are:

1. Find watermill in a location I want to live in.
2. Secure finance necessary to buy it (possibly including selling my current home).
3. Devise a cost plan for restoration using tradespeople that I trust.
4. Find a job in the new area I will be living in.
5. Buy the mill.
6. Move in and set up caravan in the garden.
7. Complete first part of restoration plan – roof, electrics, walls.
8. Complete second part of restoration plan – kitchen, bathroom.
9. Complete final part of restoration plan – decoration, carpets, furniture, garden.
10. Sit by the open fire with a cup of tea and a blanket on my knees, reading the Sunday papers.

Love Your List

The next stage is to break these key Milestones down into tasks.

A task is a more specific and smaller activity that is necessary to get you to a Milestone. You would normally have a number of small tasks that fall out of your Milestone. You will need to perform several of these to get you to a Milestone.

Tasks require a short, sharp burst of energy and are more time-bound, specific activities. Let's take the first Milestone on the list from the watermill example to see how this breaks down into manageable tasks.

Task list for Milestone 1: Find watermill in a location I want to live in.

1. Use the internet to find out where and how unusual properties are advertised.
2. Contact the Watermill Association to find out if there is a list of mills in the UK.
3. Use property search engines to discover average prices and discover what I can buy for the money I currently have.
4. Identify three local areas that hold an attraction for me.
5. Visit these key areas.
6. Join estate agents in this areas.
7. Begin posting adverts online and around the local area.
8. Identify top three properties.
9. Decide on one.

You can see from this list that some of the tasks are going to take longer than others. Some are totally within your control – fact-finding and research, while others are less in your control – what is available and at what price. The tasks are also going to take variable amounts of effort.

Despite this absence of control over all the factors involved, you do have a degree of influence. You can put forth a lot of effort to help make what you want to happen occur. The funny thing is, that on some level, the Universe rewards action. As long as you keep taking action with the intention to experience what you desire, you will be rewarded.

It Takes As Long As It Takes

Despite our lack of total control, it is still helpful to make some estimates around time. These may need revising as we embark on the Quest. Some things may happen much faster than we expect, while others may seem to take forever.

I suggest that you start by putting in an end date for the completion of the Quest.

For example, by Autumn 2014, I will be holding my adopted child in my arms in our garden at home.

By figuring out an end date, you can then revisit each Milestone and know when it will need to be completed by in order to keep on track. By reviewing from the first Milestone to the last, you can get some indication of the duration of your Quest.

You will need to take a realistic look at the shape of your life. This includes the hours and days that you have free to focus on the Quest. Taking some measure of the realistic amount of time you can dedicate to this project will also help you to make a reasonable time estimate.

Say I have five hours a week to dedicate to Project Watermill. I can look at my list of tasks for my first Milestone and know that this is not going to get done in a week. Or even four weeks. Three months looks more likely to me.

Making Your Own Project Plan

Remind yourself of the outcome of your Quest, your ultimate destination.

Remind yourself of where you are now in relation to your Quest.

What are the key Milestones you need to reach? Can you find a tangible or quantifiable measure for these Milestones? It could be distance travelled, number of days sober, people contacted, material or location found.

Now, start with your first Milestone and break this down into bite-size tasks. Don't be afraid to make these really small or short. The more manageable they are, the more confident you will feel about your ability to do them.

Looking at your Milestone again – is there a date by which this needs to be accomplished? If there isn't a line in the sand, I suggest you draw one. Look at your task list. Make an estimate of how long each task could take.

Now look at your life. How much time do you have each week for your Quest? Ten minutes a day? All day every day? This will influence your timeline.

My friends Christo and Mat are major film buffs. In 2006 they moved their community cinema project to a purpose-built venue in the Stepney Bank area of Newcastle. The time and effort to realize their vision was way beyond what two fellas could achieve. How then do you build a custom-made community cinema space on an £18,000 budget? You enlist 100 volunteers to build it with you! Many hands make light work. The Star and Shadow is a community-owned "nursery for independent and creative thinking." It's run entirely by volunteers (see www. Starandshadow.org.uk.)

Follow the Yellow Brick Road

In the Wizard of Oz, Dorothy finds herself and her dog have arrived in a whole new world. Together with her magical friends, Scarecrow, Tin Man and the Cowardly Lion, Dorothy begins her Quest by following the Yellow Brick Road, the path that will lead them to the Wizard who has the ability to grant all their wishes. Tin Man wants a heart, the Cowardly Lion wants courage and Scarecrow wants a brain. Dorothy just wants to get home.

The yellow brick road of your Quest is known in project management as the "critical path." This path maps out the things that must happen, in a certain order, for your Quest to be successful. For example, one cannot give birth without pregnancy. There are a variety of ways to become pregnant beyond the traditional horizontal method, but currently, only pregnancy can result in giving birth.

Your critical path is important because it stops you getting stuck on things that are not critical to your success. It also helps to highlight when and where you are procrastinating or dithering. I once had a client who was a holistic therapist. She had created a lovely space in her home and had taken all sorts of qualifications to be able to offer a great service to her potential clients. Trouble was, we couldn't get her any clients because she had no marketing material to give them. Why? Because she became obsessed with the colour to use on her logo and would not print anything or complete her website until she had decided on it. No marketing, no clients. The fact that the colours could be changed further down the line did not seem to click with her. So we stalled because of a perfectionistic detail.

Perfection is the enemy of good

When you look at your task list, for each Milestone try to challenge yourself about what level each task needs to be done at and whether it actually needs to be done at all. You can divide your tasks into Must, Should or Could:

- Must tasks are critical path actions – nothing will happen without them.
- Should tasks are "good to haves."
- Could tasks are enjoyable luxuries.

Start With the End in Mind

Stephen Covey, author of the book, *The Seven Habits of Highly Effective People*, talks about starting with the end in mind. This technique of "imaginary hindsight" helps us tap into the more intuitive and creative part of our brain. We do this by imagining that we have already achieved our Quest and looking back to the present to see the yellow brick road we took.

Here's the outline for starting at the end and working backwards. You will need to begin by projecting yourself into the future. Imagine your Quest was achieved and completed. How do you feel and how is the world different to now? From that perspective, let's look at the steps you took to get there.

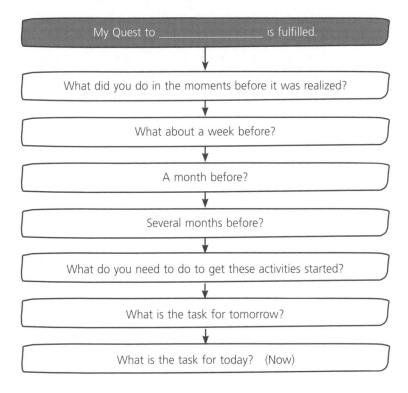

My Quest to _____ is fulfilled.

What did you do in the moments before it was realized?

What about a week before?

A month before?

Several months before?

What do you need to do to get these activities started?

What is the task for tomorrow?

What is the task for today?   (Now)

Standing on the Shoulders of Giants

If you are feeling a bit worried about how on earth you are going to get clear on the next steps in your Quest, fear not! There is an incredible resource available to you for free, or almost free, that you can tap into to get inspiration, guidance and answers.

What's that you ask? Where is it? How can I get some?

Well, it's all around you in the form of the stories and experiences of other people!

Research who has gone before on this kind of a Quest.

Find the pioneers. What route did they take traversing the Matterhorn? What kind of diet did they use to help them get back to peak fitness? How did they start their business on a shoestring budget?

You can find out what their mistakes were, benefit from their hindsight and take their shortcuts. How good is that?
All of this information is now available in a huge variety of forms.

- Listen to talks.
- Download lectures or podcasts.
- Find articles or press cuttings about them.
- Visit their website.

Note: Please don't alarm your inspiring role models – we want to win their support and time, not have them call the police to report suspicious activity! Be creative in attracting their attention AND be respectful.

What immediate research will you commit to?

Who do you know who could help you with this?

Risk Management

Questing folk do funny things with their heads. When I work with them, I often discover that they are living in fear of an imagined cataclysmic disaster. When we store up anxieties and fears about what could happen, we divert energy from where it needs to be focused – on the positive action we need to take. Our sense of aversion to risk can, at worst, leave us totally paralyzed. Putting together a risk log is one way to keeping your focus positive and your mind calm. A well-researched plan is the best defense against any of the risks and obstacles that will occur on the way through your Quest.

Your risk log

- Write down the absolutely worst thing that could happen if you embark on your Quest and start heading toward your first Milestone. Really go for it in capturing your worst case scenario. Make sure you capture all the anxieties that your Inner Family can think of.
- Rate these risks on a scale of 1 to 10. You are going to rate them for the likelihood that they will occur, and the severity of the impact on you or your Quest if they did occur. The BP oil rig disaster was very unlikely and it was also very serious. Finding you have little in common with a person you have never met may be a bit more likely, but it is a lot less serious. Rating scales enable you to ground your fear in a bit more reality.

How likely is it to happen?

How serious would it be if it did happen?

- Now your next question needs to be about the fundamental fear – that of loss of your life or the lives of others. It will be rare that the answer to this is yes, but sometimes, if we are planning a very significant adventure, it can be life or death.

Would you survive if the worst happened?

If the answer is no, you will of course need to look at some very serious considerations and risk mitigation. Adventurers do sometimes lose their lives. Chris McCandless, whose story is told in the book, *Into the Wild*, was a young adventurer who wanted to experience living in total isolation for a period. He was not well prepared, but did have experience of living rough. His main follies were not having a map and not being able to call or alert others in case of emergency. A few days before he decided to leave the shelter where he had been living for 113 days, he died from accidental poisoning from some berries he had eaten. A risk log could have literally saved his life.

Whether our risk is likely to be fatal or not, we need to consider what we can do to reduce the risk occurring. This is called "mitigating" the risk. We also need to look at what our Plan B would be if the worst did happen. Is there anything you can put in place to reduce the severity of that impact?

Complete your risk log here.

- Mitigation of Risk . . .
- Plan B . . .

A common fear of someone going self-employed might be that they would have no customers or not enough customers.

Here is an example from a person trying out a new treatment for a life threatening illness:

Risk	Likelihood	Severity	Mitigation	Plan B
The medicine makes me even more weak	4/10	7/10	Look at the research on this drug, evaluate alternatives, talk to my family about it before any final decision is made.	Plan B – ask partner to see if they can get some flexibility at work to care for me during the trial, see if there are any supplements I can take to support me.

I recommend that you use your risk log at least weekly. You can keep adding as new opportunities or concerns crop up. This means these worries no longer live in your head and you have more perspective over them and can take constructive action. Eco-activist Marina Pepper on a very lonely meeting:

"One of the worst things that can happen to an activist is to call a meeting and be the only person who turns up. Then you have to have a meeting with yourself that goes – either there is something wrong with my cause or there is something wrong in the way I went about organising it, like an inconvenient or clashing time, or forgetting to publish the date and venue . . . Either way, you learn from your worst case, for sure."

What Is Your Immediate Next Step?

So now we have a map to your Quest and a better understanding of the risks, a bird's eye view of the overarching journey and the steps and milestones along the way. Now we need to begin to put one foot in front of the other and to keep ticking off our tasks until they add up to a Milestone where we can stop to review, reflect and mark our progress. In the olden days, we could chart progress by the stars, the number of full moons or by marking scratches on a stone wall. Now we can let the world share in our progress via a blog or by using all manner of programmes to help us keep track of progress in the form of the Quantified Self movement.

Quantified Self is a new term for the different digital devices and electronic apps that we can use to keep tabs on our behaviour. There is an extraordinary range available, from the humble calendar and task list, to apps that track your eating or walking, time spent off the grid.

Quantified Self Apps

- Fit Bit – tracks your activity and sleep patterns.
- DigiFit – tracks the speed and cadence of your athletic efforts.
- Mood Panda – tracks your happiness and identifies the reasons why.
- Zeo – the personal sleep coach.

Another great way to track progress is through visual boards that sit around your home or office showing you how far you have come in relation to your goal. They could be gold stars, images, graphs – anything that gives you, and others involved in your Quest, a sense of your momentum and progress.

Celebrating Success

The part of us that is motivated to get things done is quite a young member of the Inner Family. This naïve character powers our motivation engine for pretty much anything we decide we want to do. It has no opinion on whether the task is realistic, good for us or even humanly possible, it just takes instructions. Imagine a five-year-old version of yourself, with a wind-up key in the back. You tell it, "I want to run a marathon and train every day" and it goes "Sure," winds up its motor and gets going. This little motivating motor, like most of the children I know, likes prizes and rewards. It wants applause, recognition, glory and treats. It is the reason why Alan Sugar gives a "treat" to the successful team on the TV show, *The Apprentice* and why they often punch the sky when they hear about it. We all like to be recognized for our achievements. Most importantly, we need to have our own self-approval and self-regard.

When we are trudging along the route to our Quest, seeing how long the road looks ahead, we can easily forget to recognize and celebrate success along the way. Trying something new, stepping into a room where you know no one, taking the first step to talk about something that is very personal to you – all these are feats that deserve reward and celebration. "A spoonful of sugar," as the magical nanny Mary Poppins might say, helps make difficult or challenging tasks a lot easier.

If you are not so hot on giving yourself acknowledgement, try these playful ways of recognizing yourself.

1. Download a soundtrack of applause. Play it for five minutes every day. Get into the habit of accepting the applause as though you were at an award ceremony.
2. Take a bow. Even if there is no audience, if you do something worthy of your own acknowledgement, perform a little bow or curtsey. Sounds silly, works every time.
3. Give yourself a certificate or a small reward like a massage or deluxe coffee. If money is tight, "Firsts" or "Brilliant Me" lists compiled every evening will provide a well-deserved pat on the back. If you would like to, you can broadcast your success, via social media or your own Quest blog.

4. Lastly, consider setting up your own Questers group or pair up with someone else who is also working through this book. You can offer each other support and mentoring as well as cheerleading one another on.

5. Email me and tell me about your achievements!

Mind the Gaps

Now that you have a fairly comprehensive picture of your Quest and the steps you will want to take to get there, it should be easier to see what is missing. If we have a recipe, it is easy for us to see which ingredients we need to pop out and buy.

No one is going to be perfectly equipped with everything they need. If you were, you would have probably completed your Quest by now. There will be something you will need to add to the mix. It could be a process or system that you need to design, an object or product that you need to make or find, or a way of presenting or sharing your ideas. The list may include skills that you need to obtain for yourself or that you wish to access through other people.

A friend of mine made it a Quest to leave a job he hated to become a solicitor. He was in his mid-thirties when he began the process of a part-time law conversion. He then started a part-time degree and finally did his practice exams. He now works as the local criminal solicitor in a market town and could not be happier. Time taken on Quest from start to finish – seven years in total. Aside from the qualifications themselves, he needed to juggle a full-time job, student loans and finance and devise for himself a rigorous plan for revision and essay writing around his full-time work. This is Questing energy and spirit. You don't have to have everything you need to hand but you do need to do everything you can to play your part in the adventure.

- Given your image of a successful outcome to your Quest, what do you now see is missing?
- What action will you take to fill in the gaps?

(Gaps include: skills, knowledge, money, process, time, tools and people)

With a plan in place and an awareness of the risks, it's time to draw in your supporters and collaborators and win them over to your team. Well done for completing your plan – be generous with the applause!

 Chapter Summary

- Every Quest needs a plan.

- The best way to plan is to break things down and make each segment manageable.

- Knowing where you want to get to at each stage helps to measure and track success.

- Progress is not about perfection – it is about "good enough to keep going."

- Managing risk helps us feel less scared about facing our trial.

- Part of planning is recognizing our gaps and learning to fill them.

- Every hero deserves their successes celebrated – you can share these or just run your own private party!

8

BUILDING YOUR DREAM TEAM

*" The key is to keep company
only with people who uplift you,
whose presence calls forth your best. "*
Epictetus

Now you have a life plan! Your next step is to enroll others in helping you make it happen. Quests are usually not small endeavours. A Big Top cannot be raised by just one person. They need collaborators who join, inspired by the aim and mission, who bring their unique talents to the party. This engagement with your Quest may come in many forms and at different times. Participation in the team may last just an afternoon when someone proves a perfect fit for a very specific task. Others may come on board for the duration, sharing an equal level of commitment for the Quest itself.

Harry Potter is perhaps the most well-known fantasy hero of our time. Each of the Harry Potter films focuses on a different battle, with the same enemy, Voldemort. Ultimately, the battle with Voldemort is Harry's gig. It's personal. They are uniquely connected. Harry's friends, Ron and Hermione, play very valuable sidekick roles and bring their own skills to bear. His mentor is Dumbledore the Wizard, who provides key insight into Harry's own abilities, reminds Harry who he is and helps him navigate the situations in which he finds himself. Along the way, Harry receives a lot of different support from varied and sometimes surprising sources.

Ultimately, as the hero in your own story, you may be on a Quest that will require you to face your Supreme Ordeal alone. But mentors, teachers, guides, gurus, friends, experts, volunteers, champions and partners, are all advisers that can play crucial roles in helping you to get to the point where you are ready to raise your lightsaber.

Many heads are better than just one. Even if there is a significant brain in there, you are limited by the way you see and experience the world. You will feel down, be lost and get muddled along the way. You will wonder why you ever started. At these times, the ability to draw energy and strength from others will be invaluable. Groups unleash creativity. Though the final decisions are likely to rest with you, having the input of others usually brings forth a much better result. It's time to find and establish your heroic dream team.

Better Together

Underneath the pinnacle on which a visible hero stands, are a large number of folk forming a strong base to the pyramid. *Dexter* is an award-winning TV drama about a serial killer. We might think that what makes the show so exceptional is its most visible parts, like the talent of Michael C. Hall, the actor who plays the eponymous lead role. Or we might attribute the success to the fabulous writing of James Manos, Jr. and his team, who adapted Jeff Lindsay's novels for TV. When I watched the "special features" section of the *Dexter* DVDs it became clear that what makes *Dexter* so special is that everyone, from sound effects to art direction, actors to writers, share a dedication to excellence. There was real pride at every stage of the chain, with everyone playing their part to make sure that what they passed on to the next stage of the process was as good as it could possibly be. More than that, there was real trust that within the team, the others could be relied on to do a great job.

The same is true of the book you have in your hands now. OK, I put the words down, scripted the idea and did my research. But in order for you to be reading this a team of designers, illustrators, editors, publishers, distributors, buyers and sellers needed to be in place to get these words to you. And before them came teachers, participants on workshops, coaching clients, patient other halves, friends and family. Everyone, consciously or unconsciously aligned to play their part and delivered to their best ability.

Teams Can Be Made Up of Competitors

Even seemingly competing elements or mortal enemies may unite around a common threat or opportunity in order to win big or to do together what they cannot do alone. There is a theory in international relations concerning collaboration across nations. It is called The Stag Hunt. In the stag hunt, four hunters come together to kill a stag. In order for them all to be successful, they need to work together. If one of them heads off into the woods to chase a rabbit, then everyone loses. A great team made up of competitors relies upon the individual team members sacrificing a degree of short-term benefit in order for everyone to win at a larger level.

In the film, *The Magnificent Seven*, a random team of seven gunmen pull together to defeat a group of bandits who are terrorizing an impoverished Mexican village. They are a diverse group of characters with a variety of motivations for taking part and share only their common skill set as gunslingers. Each member of the team goes through their individual Hero's Journey as they unite against the common enemy. However, things quickly fall apart once their immediate objectives are completed.

Collaboration takes trust and it doesn't always come easily. But when it happens, it is a beautiful thing to witness. In 2010–11, Manchester United commenced an extraordinary winning streak. Watching the early part of each match, they seemed disjointed, lacking in confidence and you would wonder whether this team were out of luck. Then, suddenly, something would click in, the whole team would function as a powerful, intuitive whole and magic would occur on the pitch.

What Kind of Support Do You Need?

In leadership speak, we talk about three ways of connecting with others. Through the heart, the hands and the head. These three categories can be used to help understand what help you may need to request at different stages of your Quest.

The Heart Team

Every hero needs some kind of emotional support at some point on the Quest, by virtue of being human. Emotional and spiritual support is given by team members who care for you and your wellbeing. They are the members of the team with whom you can most be yourself. They might be family and friends, pastors, spiritual advisers, coaches or counsellors. These team members help keep you balanced and spiritually healthy. They offer a shoulder to cry on, a listening ear, hugs and tea as needed, and help pick you up when all you want to do is throw in the towel. Their love and support for you is unconditional. If you have a spiritual practice or faith, your Higher Power and congregational community come under this banner.

The All-Hands-to-the-Pump Team

These are the crew on the ship. Your partners in crime. Practical support comes in the form of hands on deck. These are the team members who provide day-to-day operational support for things you need help with. They could bring any number of different talents depending on the stage of the Quest you are on and the types of skills required for the project as a whole. They might be writers, thinkers, technicians, administrators, carers, fundraisers, marketeers, window cleaners, stilt walkers, the list is endless. They enable the Quest to get up and running.

I recently attended the Shambala festival, one of a number of wonderful festivals that have sprung up in the English countryside in recent years. I am particularly fond of Shambala because of the very special atmosphere it creates. This is a combination of a beautiful environment, a certain quirky and playful culture and, most of all, a ratio of one festival team member for every five revellers. That's a better ratio than most classrooms!

A team of people that straddle the Heart and the Head are your peer group. These are the individuals out there who are on a similar Quest. They may play the same role as you in a different industry. They may be striving for a similar goal. Your peer group can give advice, direct you to resources or help you plan your next step.

The Boffins, Experts and Gurus Team

Expert support takes the form of mentors, gurus, campaign specialists, advisers and technical specialists. These might be teachers, doctors, lawyers, strategists, designers or anyone with a particular skill set that you need filled for a specific and time-bound period. Experts tend to be like luxury chocolate truffles, you might have a little of them now and then and they are unlikely to be part of the day-to-day, but their knowledge and experience are crucial at specific points on the journey.

It's the moment to consolidate your thinking on your dream team. Below is a table capturing different stages of the Quest. Take some time to consider the type of support you may need at each stage.

Stages	Research and Planning	Starting Up	Going Forward	Completion
Kinds of Support				
Heart				
Hands				
Heads				

- Which of the three types of support do you most need at the start of this Quest?
- Do you have people in mind to fill these team roles?

The Best Ways to Find Your Dream Team

The Heart of the Matter

The emotional support team search is a fairly simple one. You are going to look to the people in your life that you trust and who love you. If these feel in short supply, you may wish to reach out to a support group – either face-to-face or online.

Finding Your Peer Group

A heroic change in direction, focus or attitude is going to need reinforcing. Few heroes wake up suddenly with a different head on. If your Quest awakens in you a new possibility for how life can be, it will be important for you to have this reinforced by peers who support and believe in it. The internet has revolutionized our level of contact with others who share our experiences. If you are going to step into the unfamiliar, you will need to explore spending time with people who understand and support your Quest. No matter where you are in the world, you are likely to be able to get online and connect with others who share your new interest, passion and need, and can offer support, counsel and community. This doesn't mean deserting friends and family. It does mean investing in a network that will be able to help you take the steps into who you want to be rather than staying with who you have been. This can be fun and eye opening – as well as giving you a whole new peer group to call on when things get tough.

The Doers

You can find great doers in a wide range of ways. The first place to check is amongst friends and family to see if they know of anyone, or if they can lend a hand. A word of caution – sometimes working with friends and family can be more tricky than collaborating with someone a little more distant from your personal life. Both can work really well, but it is just something to be mindful of.

Alongside your personal networks, you might find support from people you currently or previously worked with. This network is often interested in your next steps and plans, so don't be afraid to let them know who you are looking for.

As well as asking friends and colleagues who they might recommend, remember to access the internet where forums on your area of interest such as www.moneysavingexpert.com, or related to your personal circumstances such as www.mumsnet.com, can extend your network globally and nationally.

Practical support also includes your "partners in crime." In order for your Quest to get off the ground you may need to find yourself a key partner who is a yin to your yang. For example, many creative people will benefit from working with a more structured and strategic mind. A great way to find a Friar Tuck to your Robin Hood is through networking. The word may cause you to come out in hives with traumatic memories concerning nibbles and monologuing accountants, but nowadays peer-to-peer networking has become popular, with websites such as meetup.com providing mutual interest groups that are free to join. In addition, professional bodies relating to your areas of passion, such as the British Library UK Entrepreneur Network Group, the RSA (Royal Society for the encouragement of Arts, Manufactures and Commerce) and the Association for Coaching often host their own events. These events are a great way to meet with people outside your normal comfort zone or from different industries. One event I went to, the Mini Bar, helped me to get to know experts in the tech environment really quickly, saving lots of time and energy.

If you are looking for part-time support with skills such as admin, childcare, marketing and accounting, you might consider using a free ads website such as www.gumtree.com or placing an ad in the local paper. There are many people out there seeking part-time work that fits around their other commitments. This can be a win/win for you both.

The Experts

II On many long journeys have I gone.
And waited, too, for others to return
from journeys of their own. Some return;
some are broken; some come back
so different only their names remain. *II*
Yoda, Star Wars

Finding an expert takes a little care and attention, particularly as experts tend to command quite high fees for their time. A great way to obtain expert advice on a subject for little cost, is to find yourself a mentor. You may have come across someone during your research who really inspired you and seemed to have what you are Questing after. Aside from your Quest research work you may also want to use online networking site, LinkedIn, to find inspiring experts with whom you can connect. I've found that a LinkedIn email to a person of influence tends to be more likely to receive a response than one to their standard email. By far the best way to get access to a great mentor though, is through an introduction or by meeting face-to-face. What's in it for them? The chance to pass on and share what they know and the opportunity to help someone grow. To impress them you will need to find a special and unique way to attract their attention letting them know that only they will do.

Who would be your dream-come-true mentor?

What heroic level of action would you be willing to take to capture their attention?

Ask the Experts

Experts are best found through personal recommendation by people you trust. There are also now a number of websites that enable you to check up on someone's credentials and expertise.

Some are specific to a sector, e.g. the Life Coach Directory, while others relate to a wider range of trades and professions.

The democracy and transparency of the internet means there is feedback available on almost everything, from service providers, www.checkatrade.com, to venues, www.tripadvisor.com. You can even check out a potential employer, as reviewed by previous or current employees at www.glassdoor.com.

Advisory Boards

Expert advice can also take the form of an advisory board. If you are setting up a charity or small business, you may find it useful to bring together a board with a range of expertise to provide specific input on your strategy and direction. An advisory board is basically a collection of mentors related to a range of subjects. They may possess helpful levels of influence in the local area or in your sector. They can help you stay on track and build your understanding of specific subject matter, such as the law or finance.

Creating a Connection

There's an exercise I teach to help people evaluate the quality of their listening. People sit in pairs and one person begins speaking. The other is instructed to listen as well as they possibly can. Then at an appointed time, they begin to "turn down" their listening quality, until they reach a point where they are not listening to the other person at all. The poor speaker generally finds it quite hard to keep going. The fact that "no one is out there" literally stops them in their tracks.

When we are working on something we believe in, striving for a cause, the affirmation of what we are doing can be crucial. This can happen by design or by accident. The Sunday Assembly, www.sundayassembly.com, was set up earlier this year to provide non-religious Sunday get-togethers for the public. Recognizing the value of ritual and play and the importance of people feeling connected in their local community, Sanderson Jones and Pippa Evans set up the event at Bethnal Green. The "service" includes songs and inspiring talks and gives people the chance to feel part of something. Sanderson says he knew it was a good idea when "I started to get criticism from both atheists and the religious."

Dig Out Your Pompoms

If the above team categories are the heart, head and hands, your cheerleaders are the mouth. They speak on your behalf to a much wider audience. These guys feel a connection with your Quest and will help to spread the word about what you are doing. They may be buyers, customers, audience, promoters or advocates. They like what you are doing. On some level, they share your values and wish to encourage you to continue. If you are involved in campaigning, carrying out a sponsored activity or in a business with customers, you will need to find, encourage and support this influential group.

A fan base can range from a few personal cheerleaders to a worldwide network. Fans of your work or your cause act as promoters – they let people know what you are up to and help you to make things happen through their alignment with your cause. There are many ways to build up a committed fan base, many of which have been revolutionized by the internet. Remember old school methods too – calling a face-to-face meeting, using flyers and posters, writing articles in local papers are all great ways to get your message out there. There are many opportunities to offer free talks or workshops and lots of audiences – from schools to business networks to the Women's Institute, who are always looking for inspiring speakers for their members and students.

Artists and musicians provide creative examples of how to build and nurture this incredibly valuable set of team members. For them, if there is no audience, the performance is a meaningless exercise. Lady Gaga's fans are affectionately termed her "little monsters" and at a recent concert she told them: "I cannot breathe without you." Politics is another arena in which we can learn much about bringing people along with you. The American Presidential campaigns offer a spectacular array of approaches to bring a huge range of people onside.

Social media has become a powerful force in the hero's arsenal. Websites such as Facebook, Instagram, Flickr, YouTube and Twitter let you share a point of view with as wide a community as you dare.

 How can you reach out to your fans to help them feel part of something special?

Setting up a blog has also never been easier, with websites such as WordPress and Blogger having you up and running within minutes. This global reach has revolutionized communication, but it still flourishes through good old-fashioned word of mouth. A "share" of your information or latest video on Facebook or someone's blog is just a virtual way of saying, "I like this woman" or "This is a great campaign" or "I think you would like this." If you are going to grow a network of fans for your work, you will need to provide regular, valuable communication that means something to them and adds value to their lives. In addition, don't forget the opportunity to meet people face-to-face.

 Aim high

- Do you need a spokesperson or influential supporter for your Quest?
- Who would that be?
- Who do you need to connect to in your "fan" or promoter base?
- Why would what you are doing matter to them?

Speaking from the Heart

> *"* Look inside yourself Simba. You are
> more than what you have become. You
> must take your place in the Circle of Life. *"*
> *Mufasa*, The Lion King

Supporters and fans feel a strong connection with a Quester. I know, that for myself, there are artists who I will almost always go and see if they are performing, singing or exhibiting near me. There are organizations and teachers that I would travel a long way or invest significant time to get to see. There are magazines I love reading and products I rave about because I think they are brilliant. We enjoy being part of the community of people who love *James Bond* films, dance jive, follow a lifestyle blog, sponsored such and such a person etc. We like to belong. If your Quest causes people to wish to align or belong to a community, this is something to be celebrated, encouraged and treasured.

We are all connected. The hero knows and understands the interdependence between himself and all others. In the trials of the Supreme Ordeal, this sense of connection is a powerful ally.

Stop. Connect. Reflect. Close your eyes and breathe. Try to sink into yourself. Feel the connections between you and others radiate out like little threads from your middle.

 Consider these key questions

- How can I serve?
- How can I give this group of people the very best of me?
- How can I take care of them and be of use?
- What would they like that I can give?
- And how can I make it fun?

" I just think that attentiveness and politeness
are so important. My fans love to know a bit
about my personal life too and, though I have
to be careful about boundaries, I do try to share
in that way. I spend a lot of time tweeting and
blogging because it is a great way of giving back
to fans and including them in the adventure. *"*
*Professor Elemental, on the power of online
networks*

If you need to raise funds for your Quest, you can try using
crowdfunding websites such as www.buzzbnk.org and www
.crowdfunder.com to build both a fan base and the money to make
a plan happen.

These websites work through you telling a powerful story about
what you want to do and offering an exchange of benefits or services with the public, in return for funding your endeavour. Sica, the
young film maker, raised £2000 this way.

Many musicians, artists and start-ups have benefited from crowdfunding. If your cause is charitable, you can do much the same
through websites such as www.justgiving.com which provide a
good platform for your "call to action."

You can help this process along by sharing a clear, simple vision.

Everyone in the team needs a simple and clear message about who
you are and what you are about. This makes it easy for fans to pass
on the good news and helps keep everyone working powerfully
together.

Now you need to have a go at structuring your message. The following exercise offers an order for your key messages to cheerleaders, supporters or mentors.

Exercise

- I (name)_____ am going to (name Quest)_____.

- I believe I am the person to do this because (explain the call) _____. The benefit of this quest for myself/others will be (complete using inspiring adjectives) _____.

- My next steps are to (headlines of the plan) _____. I know there is no way I can do this on my own. To get to the end goal, I am going to need support in the form of (name needs) _____.

- I would like to ask you as (expert/friend/mentor) to help me (name task)_____.

- It would be great to have you on side and I would love you on my team because (name genuine reasons)_____ _____. You might enjoy collaborating because (name what's in it for them)_____.

- Whaddaya say?

Commitment: No Matter What

Ernest Shackleton, a polar explorer who undertook a heroic expedition in the early 1900s is still seen as the poster boy of people-centred leadership. His Quest began in October 1908, when he and his team began "The Great Southern Journey" to visit the furthest reaches of the southern hemisphere. With trials including near starvation rations, the loss of their ship and the extreme conditions, Shackleton was nevertheless determined that everyone would make it back safely. In a race against the clock and as supplies dwindled, he continued to keep his team cohesive and their mood determined and elevated. He often gave away his last piece of food in order to ensure the wellbeing and morale of his team. Shackleton continues to be remembered for his courage and endurance. Recent journeys attempting to recreate his expeditions have illustrated that what he did and enabled his team to do, was indeed truly extraordinary.

Secret Sauce

So the plan of action to grow a powerful team is in place. You know who you need and have some idea how to find them. You know who you need to be and the powerful story you will need to tell to win supporters.

Now that you have built up a profile of your dream collaborators and supporters, you need to sprinkle the magic. How do you do this?

By being open to the possibility of your wish being granted.

Think about it.

How often have you approached a situation with doubts and cynicism? How often have you found yourself thinking – "This won't work" or "They don't care about me." Human beings love to share what they know. They love to be part of something. They like to connect with others. Allow yourself, in every interaction, to be curious and open-minded. To see what can come of the interaction for the benefit of everyone concerned. The secret sauce is to allow yourself to trust that it will work out, that you will connect with the right people. When you do, practice allowing yourself to receive their support, help, advice and love. This can be the hardest part. You cannot just give. You cannot just be the martyr – serving others and sacrificing endlessly. You have to learn to come with your arms open wide and receive good will and support graciously.

Your homework is to have a go at bravely asking for support in your Quest. Is there a person, a resource or an opportunity that would bring your progress on in leaps and bounds? Are you willing to be brave enough to ask for it? What is certain, is that if you don't ask, you will never get it. Write the letter to your role model asking to study with them, ask for the building, money, airplane, materials or whatever it is you need. See if you can make magic happen.

 Chapter Summary

- Most Quests will require the support and input of others – this is great news!

- There are a huge number of willing supporters, mentors and doers out there to help you.

- Many Quests will also need a voice – people who advocate or cheerlead the Quest into success.

- To win support you will need to learn how to tell a powerful story with a simple key message.

- Storytelling is a key skill for heroic endeavours and benefits both the speaker and the listener.

- The key to success in your Quest lies in learning to receive support and allowing people to get behind you.

- Challenging Quests demand the making of challenging requests.

9

THE EXTERNAL BATTLE

II No battle plan ever
survives contact with the enemy. *II*
Helmuth von Moltke

Our Life Plan is in place. Now it is time for us to put it into action. We can expect to be tested and stretched. In any story, there comes a point when the hero becomes lost in the lonely wilderness that the Hero's Journey calls "The Belly of the Whale." This is the point in your journey where you are likely to face trials. You are building up your experience and skills in preparation for the Supreme Ordeal. The next two chapters are dedicated to the exploration of the external and internal challenges we face and strategies to deal with them.

The Belly of the Whale describes the process of getting worn down and having to demonstrate your resilience and commitment to the Quest. You know you are in the belly when you have secured that longed-for promotion – but now management are coming down hard on you with targets and your boss is scary and your team hostile. You have decided to commit to the IVF process and now the daily rounds of injections, the hormonal imbalances, the scare stories and the emotional stress are starting to take their toll . . . you get the idea. The Belly of the Whale signifies that you are too far from what you left behind to turn back and yet the future looks doubtful, uncertain or plain old frightening.

This is the point at which our doubts and fear enter in, we begin to get tired and lonely. We start to wonder if the struggle is actually going to be worth it.

The Supreme Ordeal is about a defining moment or time period, where we are challenged to be more than we think we can be, where we face our demons, go up against a grand test or attempt to raise the Big Top – launching your vision into reality or into the mainstream. Your commitment is really put to the test.

The following pages provide approaches to navigate the labyrinth and develop the armour to prevent being worn down by those who oppose or criticize us along the way.

Growing Pains

II In my life I had come to realize that when things were going very well indeed it was just the time to anticipate trouble. And, conversely, I learned from pleasant experience that at the most despairing crisis, when all looked sour beyond words, some delightful 'break' was apt to lurk just around the corner. *II*
Amelia Earhart, American aviation pioneer, talking about the importance of accepting the ebb and flow of the Quest

It wouldn't make much of a story if every Quest were plain sailing. We have never, ever in the history of mankind, learned anything through something being easy. It is only in our testing times that we connect with the deeper aspects of life that we grow, stretch and are challenged to go beyond anything we have known before. It is the unfamiliar, the plunge into new and uncomfortable spaces that provide the opportunity to evolve. This awareness can support us to accept where we are and the difficulty we are in. If you are struggling, lost and confused, then you know you are exactly where you need to be! The challenges are always a darkness before the dawn. If we have faith in the nature of our Quest and the courage to keep our intention, we know that we will overcome the times when it all seems hopeless.

Critics and Naysayers

" It isn't the mountains ahead to climb that wear you out; it's the pebble in your shoe. "
Muhammad Ali

Critics and worriers can do tremendous damage to you when you are Questing. When you are taking action on your Life Plan it seems that suddenly everyone feels entitled to express their point of view on your approach. They might express doubts about its viability or "dump" their worries and anxieties on you leaving you feeling absolutely deflated and hopeless.

If this sounds familiar, do not lose heart! Taking action in a way that flows against the grain of the day-to-day is bound to incite some reaction. When we take a step toward what we want, we will often find that this makes others uncomfortable. By making a commitment to achieve what you want out of life, you are forcing them to notice the dreams and goals that they have not allowed themselves to pursue.

You may also be acting a bit strangely. Changing your routine, spouting off about your vows and taking what they see as potentially risky or dangerous action. Even those closest to you may struggle to adjust and offer their wholehearted support.

While there will be a contingent of people who feel agitated or provoked by your steps forward, there are going to be others who are inspired and energized by you. Ultimately, whether there is cheering or booing going on outside your door, Questing requires that you follow the dictates of your own conscience.

Now this is not to say that anyone who offers constructive feedback on your Quest should be greeted with "lalalala I have my fingers in my ears" behaviour. Constructive feedback, given in a non-blaming manner, can be extraordinarily helpful to a Quester. Being open to help, whatever form it might take, is a crucial skill set for you right now. Even when the approach isn't so sensitive, it is always worth us mining what has been shared to extract what is useful to us.

If you have strong critics around you, they can be useful for road testing how watertight an idea or plan is. To get the best out of their advice, you may wish to follow the following process:

1. Genuinely thank them for caring enough to share their opinion or thoughts with you.
2. Acknowledge their perspective using the words: "To you . . ." e.g. "To you, this is a madcap scheme that is not going anywhere. . ."
3. Share your point of view: "To me . . ." e.g. "To me, this is an opportunity to use my business skills and combine them with something I love, to give people a once-in-a-lifetime balloon ride across the countryside . . ." (or whatever).
4. If they simply condemn your action with no explanation, ask them for more information – if they will not provide it, then express regret, as the absence of that information means you cannot really do anything to respond intelligently to their feedback.

Differences of opinion about the fundamentals of the action you are taking will usually come down to values. Put simply, you value something more than the other person. Say you value freedom and adventure and the other person values stability and security. Neither is better than the other. Neither of you are wrong. Learning to value and appreciate different points of view and different Quests is part of the hero's destiny. Everyone has their own unique Quest. They do not need to agree with yours.

The film, *Billy Elliott*, is the story of a young boy who decides to become a ballet dancer. He stumbles across the class when it takes place in his local boxing gym where he has been sent to toughen up. His brother and father are totally outraged when they discover he wants to dance, fearing he will be branded a "poof." They eventually come round once they see him dance.

The life-denying influence can be just as powerful as the life affirming, so you do need to be careful who and what you listen to. Make sure that any negative input is countered and balanced by more measured, optimistic or inspiring voices.

You can't expect everyone to agree with you or to applaud your efforts. Different generations, values and points of view all make for different perspectives on life. You will waste a lot of energy if you prioritize getting approval over taking Questing action. But you can also find value in taking the time to explain to someone you love, what you are doing and why it matters so much to you to give it a go.

It might take a little while, but those who love you unconditionally might change their minds once they see how happy your Quest can make you.

Release Resentments

" Life appears to me too short to be spent nursing animosity or registering wrongs. *"*
Charlotte Brontë, Jane Eyre

Resentment is the feeling we get when we believe that someone else or the world itself, has wronged us. It feels like a vice and it tastes like iron. It is created by the bizarre notion that if we eat enough poison, the person we resent will drop down dead. It can eat us up.

When you hold on to your grudges toward others you waste your energy on making someone else wrong. And when you feel a victim to life itself, you make it wrong. This changes nothing. Life just happens, with all of its pains and sorrows, twists and turns. You become the destroyer if you hold on.

In the book, *Great Expectations*, by Charles Dickens, we meet Miss Havisham. Abandoned on her wedding day, she sits years later in the debris of her life. The clocks around her are all stopped at the time she heard the news. Decades on, she holds her grudge, her life on pause, still wearing the ancient wedding dress. Life froze for her when she was jilted and she remains determined to wreak her revenge on all mankind.

Does this sound familiar to you?

If this is something you know you suffer from and you know that holding this level of opposition toward someone who has hurt you is doing you more harm than good, now is the time to get out of jail. Consider forgiving the other person. That doesn't mean that you condone their action but it will stop you corroding from the inside and free your energy to focus on the present and the future. In heroic compassion, you can allow the other person to be a frail and fallible human being, just like you. You may not have liked what they did and it may have been really wrong, but they were doing the best they could with the knowledge and skills they had at the time.

Here is an exercise around resentment to play with. Try to be as specific and honest as you can about what you feel you need to forgive. And remember that a heroic approach requires compassion – the other person was doing the best they could.

Capture something that you feel resentful about here. It could be someone's behaviour, a circumstance you find yourself in, or something that was heard or said about you that you feel was unfair.

- How does the resentment make you feel? Notice it in your body.
- Would you rather have peace than this feeling?
- If you would, complete the sentence, I forgive you _____ for_____. I would rather feel peace instead of this.

Repeat this exercise until the feeling lifts.

Be a Light to Others

Your courage in claiming your life is a service to others.

Every time a hero takes a risk on their own behalf, they give others the courage to do the same.

The character Shug in Alice Walker's novel, The Color Purple, has a transformative and inspiring effect on those around her. Turning up unexpectedly amongst a group of people beaten down by their history, she is unashamedly and proudly herself. Her presence reconnects them to life and to love and helps to heal the wounds of their past. Similarly, in Jean-Pierre Jeunet's film, Amélie, the principal character has a very lonely and isolated upbringing. Her discovery of a box of forgotten childhood treasures in her rented flat sets her on a Quest to reunite them with their owner. Her eccentric ways and anonymous acts of kindness ultimately light up the lives of those around her and transform her own life.

The following exercise is designed to counter the opposition and negativity that you may face in the Belly of the Whale. We will achieve this by bringing the magic and lightness of the Quest back into your life.

Have a go at writing or drawing a metaphor for your work in the world. What image, symbol or idea speaks to how your Quest is transforming you or the world around you.

Begin the sentence with – My Quest is a bit like . . .

Examples include:

- My Quest to set up a charity for relatives of those with terminal illness, is a bit like a lighthouse. When people are confused about where to go for support, we will offer a beacon of light to guide them home.
- My Quest to publish my first book of poems is a bit like a hug. The poems will be warm, enveloping and comforting, like sitting on your grandma's knee.
- My Quest to become an award-winning dancer is a bit like being on a trampoline. Sometimes I am high and upbeat, sometimes I come crashing down, but there is always a little bounce left to help me get back up again!

Your go.

Course Correction

Course correction is what we do when we learn that our plan needs to change a little. We have to be flexible and open because things rarely go exactly according to plan.

Your Quest is like a maze. It has twists and turns. You will not always travel in a straight line from A to B. You will find obstacles, options and decision points. Sometimes the route you take will lead you to a dark, dank and smelly corner. This is, as my mother is fond of saying, "All part of the holiday fun!" Course Correction is an essential part of the journey.

Course Correction Is Normal

My other half, Peter, has an old sailing boat. When we think of sailboats, we might imagine most of them to have a wheel, like a steering wheel, to drive the thing. His has what is known as a tiller, a long handle that you use to steer the vessel in the direction you want to go in. Even in calm water, there is a constant process of course correction taking place – you focus on a point on the horizon and make adjustments accordingly to help you stay on course for that point. In bad weather, this process is all the more intense and requires real concentration. It is very easy to steer off course.

The same is true for Questing. Inevitably, things do not go exactly according to plan. When we start out, we have very limited information about the journey we are on – we can only make our best guess as to how long things will take or how easy they will be. As we move forward, we gather more data, have more experiences, meet more people, flesh out our ideas and discover alternative routes. This process of course correction can only come about through encountering obstacles and challenges. So, we welcome these as opportunities to check our course.

We can help ourselves through the use of a project review at each Milestone. We can build in opportunities to reflect, and people to reflect with, whose opinion we trust and respect.

 Decide on an approach for reviewing and Course Correction. How frequently do you need to review progress to feel safe and comfortable on your Quest? Who is the best person to do this with? Get it in the diary before you continue reading.

Embrace Your Mistakes

You can rely on the creative power of failure. Mistakes are just experiments that didn't create the result you had planned on. When you encounter obstacles, consider it a development opportunity. A chance to be more creative.

Arlene Blum is a mountaineer. She led the first all-female expedition to Annapurna in October 1978. That might have been enough of a Quest. However, in order to do it, she and the team had to raise $80,000, a huge amount of money at that time. So the Quest got extended to include becoming an entrepreneur. The climbers set up a T-shirt business and raised the funds through their memorable slogan: "A woman's place is on top." On 15 October 1978, they became the first group of women to reach the summit. The Quest was not without the risks or trials of the Supreme Ordeal. Two climbers, Alison Chadwick-Onyszkiewicz and Vera Watson, lost their lives along the way.

We have to see Questing as an iterative process. A game of trial and error. We have to develop our muscle memory, just as we would if we wanted to shoot an arrow to a target or play a complicated arpeggio. There is no way but through.

We have to trust that there is a gift for us when we end up lost. Sometimes, there is a magical and transforming opportunity behind an obstacle if we look at it the right way. Sometimes the shift in perception we are forced into, is the making of us.

So repeat after me (and feel free to punch the sky!):

All hail the mistake!
The blessed blunder!
The stumble!
The wrong turn!
Failure is the only way to grow!
I trust in the power of failure!
I embrace getting things wrong!

I own my gaffs!
I choose my gaffs!
I love my gaffs!

 Make yourself a sign. Something about it being OK to crash and burn, to get knocked down and get up again, Stick it somewhere where you will see it constantly.

The Wall

The marathon runners amongst you will be familiar with the term The Wall. The Wall is the point of full body exhaustion that marathon runners reach at around 32 kilometres. It feels as if they cannot move another step. Runners know to expect it, but that doesn't necessarily make it any easier to deal with. To avoid The Wall, runners need to take time to refuel before they burnout. If they wait until they hit The Wall, they are unlikely to be able to keep going, because the fuel they take in at that time will take time to be processed for use as energy.

Questing frequently runs the risk of burnout. Because your Quest is often all consuming, it becomes a crusade. A 24-hour endeavour. There is always more than can be done.

While you are never fully off duty on a Quest, you do still need to take some time out. You are no good to the world or to yourself if you are not able to stay in balance. There is no question that a Quest will challenge and stretch you, but heroic types must learn to find ways to take time out and recharge. Neglecting the fundamentals – sleep, food, time off with loved ones, is, and trust me on this, a recipe for disaster.

As Mr Miyagi said to young Daniel in the film, *The Karate Kid*: "Lesson not just karate only. Lesson for whole life. Whole life have a balance. Everything be better. Understand?"

This is not rocket science, but it is really important. The Quest needs you fit and well. Take time out. Integrate exercise and movement. Take care of your diet. Get emotional nourishment. Have a routine. Work hard. Keep it simple.

As you progress, you may wish to spend some time reviewing your working style. Are you a hell for leather or a slow and steady? Are you able to stay calm under pressure? What works well for you in releasing stress? To help you with this, a "fix me" list can prove very useful. This is a list of constructive and supportive tools you can use to help yourself when you do need to stop and recharge.

Good things to have on your list include:

- A bath.
- A good book.
- A walk in nature.
- Watching a film or your favourite DVD.
- Taking a creative class.
- A phone call with a friend.
- A face-to-face chat with a loved one.
- Practicing a hobby – gardening, music, craftwork.
- Writing in your journal.
- Going out to an event, a show, a gig, a gallery or an exhibition.

Make your list here.

What self-care practices do you need to put in place?

What if I Really Am Heading for Disaster?

I am a big believer in that what is meant to be will come to pass one way or another. What is for you will not go past you. It might take longer than you had hoped, it might cost a lot more than you thought financially or emotionally and it may look quite different to how you expect, but if your intention is clear and you take the right steps, you will get to your goal.

Occasionally, I work with someone who really seems to be chasing the wrong dream or the wrong goal. They are just exhausted. Beaten. Frustrated. The world seems to be against them and the fulfillment of their Quest. If this is where you find yourself, there are three things that could be happening.

1. This is not your choice of Quest. You are doing it for someone else or to make someone else happy. A Quest that is not your own requires ignoring the Quest that is your true Calling. This always costs us dearly until we listen.
2. There is something wrong with the way you are approaching the problem. Look at your approach. Have you kept your thinking fresh? Tried a number of different ways to get to your goals? Refined your strategy in the light of feedback? Or, when the world tells you that something is not working and you need to try something different, are you digging your heels in and refusing to change? We know it's madness to continue doing something that we know doesn't work. Looking at our objective differently can open up new choices and options. We saw this when Montezuma's ended up manufacturing chocolate.
3. There are other choices to make that would give you a different outcome, you just aren't willing to take them. These may include delay/postponement, a radical change of approach, a partnership or a different route to the same goal. The film, *127 Hours*, tells the true story of Aron Ralston, an outdoor enthusiast, who slipped and fell into a crevasse. As he fell, he dislodged a boulder which trapped and crushed his arm, pinning him against the crevasse wall. Five days later and after futile attempts to chip away at the stone with his utility knife, he was forced to break and then cut off his own arm using the, by now, blunt knife, in order to escape. Ralston recounts the story in his autobiography, *Between a Rock and a Hard Place*, saying: "I didn't lose my hand, I gained my life back."

Your solution may not require you to lose a limb, but if you really feel you have got yourself into a pickle, you are going to need to take a step back, take a deep breath and conduct a Course Correcting review.

Yikes, I Didn't See That One Coming

Sometimes the Quest opens up a can of worms. You think you are en route to your target and then discover that to get there, you are going to need to accomplish a whole new set of goals in order to take your next step.

J.K. Rowling talks about this in relation to her book, *Harry Potter and the Goblet of Fire*. There she was, cantering toward the end of her Quest with the submission of the book to the publisher, when suddenly, she discovered a large hole in the plot. An unravelled thread of story that would require hundreds of extra pages to tie up.

> *II* I got halfway through my plans and realized there was a huge gaping plot hole – it just didn't meet. It was entirely my own fault. I should have had the good sense to go through my plan very, very carefully before I started writing but I hadn't. *II*
> *J.K. Rowling, on how she could not cheat her readers*

Rowling had to go back and remove an entire character. Although she got there in the end, the reworking of the book meant missing the deadline by two months.

Learn to Love Your Lessons

So we know that the way will be fraught with challenges, tests and trials. We will use all our resources, stretch our intellect, skill and energy to the limit. The heroic response to all of this . . . accept it as though you chose it.

Because you know, the truth is, that you did. You signed up to it. And if you did your research and went in with your eyes open, you had a pretty good idea of how it could go. Every mother who has ever borne a child knows that birth can kill you. It frequently did in the past and still does sometimes today. Any parent who has ever raised a child knows the agony they set themselves up for should that child get ill, lost or die before their time. Every artist knows that along the path to success there will be ridicule, writer's block, the risk of poverty and periods of no work.

Accepting our circumstances as though we chose them creates an interesting dynamic inside. Once we realize that this is a situation we have chosen to experience, we feel a little more powerful. And when we feel a little more powerful, we become more able to look on the bright side. Even the experience of addiction can serve as a useful teacher.

Pamela, a client of mine who overcame alcoholism so bad that she was told she could lose her life, provides an exceptional example of this:

> "My addiction was the best thing that ever happened to me. Somehow, I have been an 'all or nothing' person since the year dot. I need things to get really bad before I will bother. And they did. I really messed myself up. But the experience of recovery, what I know about myself now. The inspiration I can be to others. My addiction was the making of me."

Questing teaches us to enjoy the challenge. You learn that you can be doing something really tough and still have a great time doing it because you are on your way. You are on point. You have a Life Plan.

II Far away there in the sunshine are my
highest aspirations. I may not reach them,
but I can look up and see their beauty, believe
in them and try to follow where they lead. *II*
Louisa May Alcott

How You Respond to the Issue, Is the Issue

We cannot control everything that happens in our life. We cannot control the environment, the economy, the weather, the laws of nature or other people. Life just happens. Our only choice point is how we respond to it. We can shake our fists, we can close ourselves off, we can get mad. All of these are choices. Whether you think yourself trapped by these inevitable challenges or see these as opportunities, will determine how you feel about it. How you feel about your circumstances will determine the number of choices you have available to you and will therefore determine how you act. Fury and resistance narrow our focus. We develop tunnel vision under stress – our eyes actually see less to left and right than they are capable of. Therefore our ability to stay calm and open, literally gives us a wider perspective and more choices.

Your Quest may turn out to be all about how you respond when you do not get what you want. How you cope when life has brought you to your knees. When we surrender to our experience and stop fighting, we create the possibility of genuine transformation.

It is, as Bob Dylan once remarked, "only after we have lost everything, that we are free to do anything."

When your back is against the wall, when it feels too much to continue, I want you to remember one tool. You are going to close your eyes, focus all of your attention on your perceived challenge and ask:

How can I see this differently?

Wait. Your answer will come.

Keep Turning Up

> **"** Nothing in this world can take the place of persistence. Talent will not; nothing is more common than unsuccessful people with talent. Genius will not; unrewarded genius is almost a proverb. Education will not; the world is full of educated failures. Persistence and determination alone are omnipotent. **"**
> *Calvin Coolidge, the thirtieth President of the United States*

It is important to keep turning up. No matter what happens, no matter whether you feel like it or not, you have got to keep showing up for your Quest. The writer must turn up at the page, the athlete at the track early in the morning, the activist at the protest. Turning up, no matter what, demonstrates your commitment to yourself and your cause. Like the psychological battle about going to the gym, or not having a cigarette or not calling your ex – it is the turning up anyway that rebuilds our sense of faith and purpose. Each little step we take in the right direction reinforces our esteem and our commitment. Until one day we look up and we are at the top of the mountain, with the world at our feet.

The environment may really be quite hostile for what you want to do. The existing structures, the political or social set up may not support your intention. Are you going to carry on regardless?

In film, *The Pursuit of Happyness*, we learn the true story of Chris Gardner. Chris is offered a life-changing opportunity as an intern at an investment bank. Only he has a five-year-old son to take care of and nowhere to stay. He has to hide the reality of his life and remain presentable and focused to achieve his Quest of a full-time job. The film is littered with his creative thinking. Instead of becoming overwhelmed by the situation he is in, he consistently steps up and goes to extraordinary lengths to meet all his responsibilities. At one point he sleeps in the bathroom of a train station because he really has nowhere else to go. He is ultimately rewarded with the role. In Chris Gardner's own words:

> "Don't ever let someone tell you that you can't do something. Not even me. You got a dream, you got to protect it. You want something, you go get it. Period."

Novak Djokovic, the top-notch tennis player, told his parents at the age of six that he planned to become the world number one. Five years later, his home in Belgrade was bombed by NATO. Long nights were spent cowering in the dark in the bomb shelter, praying, but during the day, he kept up his tennis, practising on courts battered by warfare.

Are you willing to do whatever it takes to achieve your goal?

Whilst in the midst of the Challenge stage, it is inevitable that there will be obstacles, disappointments, and difficulties to overcome. You can choose to see these as the deliberate choices of an unkind God or the unfairness of life – and this will leave you feeling very powerless in relation to them. Or, you can choose to see these as trials and tests of your commitment – are you going to get where you need to go – no matter what?

Now is the time to confirm to yourself your absolute commitment. To remember your intention. Your goal. Your vow. You are not going to take no for an answer. You are not going to let this one slide. We all need some fighting talk. This is your time for your own motivational speech. Be your own rousing motivational speaker. I want to hear you roar!

Chapter Summary

- It is important to know your own mind and to protect your vision from the damage of critics.

- Letting go of resentment toward other people can free up your energy.

- Every plan will need Course Correction.

- Sometimes a change of plan can give you an even better result, so stay flexible.

- Mistakes are learning opportunities to be embraced.

- When you are on the right path, even the hardest tasks can feel like fun.

- Remember to take care of yourself along the way.

- Go all out for what you want.

10

THE INTERNAL BATTLE

" Often there will be nothing you need to do about your private feelings. They don't have to be acted on. Or run away from. Or turned into something else. They don't have to be turned on someone else. They are just part of what makes you human in your own unique way. "
Susie Orbach, On Eating

The hardest, scariest battles are the ones we wage with ourselves. There is no bigger demon than our own fears and judgements. This is what the much misused word "jihad" or holy war, actually refers to. The battle between light and dark that rages inside of us. The head-on clash between our positive sense of self and our own negativity. This sense of limitation impacts almost everyone. And the more you care, the more your Quest matters to you, the more likely you are to occasionally feel overwhelmed by your internal demons. Many talented people have struggled with their mental health. Indeed here seems to be a connection between the energy of creation and instability in our inner world.

As you move toward your Supreme Ordeal, it can feel exhausting. The journey seems to have gone on forever. In the final stages of the Quest, it is absolutely normal and natural to struggle with your demons. You seem so far from the start line – so far from the safety of the familiar. And yet the destination you long to see, the vision you have invested so much in, still seems very far away. Perhaps you begin to wonder if it is even a real possibility. Perhaps you fear your destination is a fantasy or a mirage.

These fears are not unfounded. It may not work. You may not be recognized. You may not get what you want. This uncertainty is the very nature of the Quest. Or, to paraphrase Joseph Campbell, "You may discover that you are at the top of the ladder, but that it is leaning against the wrong wall."

So you are right to be concerned that your life, liberty and state of mind are at stake. Sometimes, the best that we can do is literally make it through the day. As my dear friend and fellow creative, Hannah, shared with me, "Erica, there are days when the inner world is so painful and exhausting that the very best you can accomplish is simply to keep breathing until it is time to go to bed."

This chapter is about those days and times. Those moments when you need to deal with guilt, resentment, fear or doubt. We will look at how to recover lost confidence and rebuild motivation. We will examine what we need to do to keep our faith that this is only the darkness before the dawn.

Facing Your Fear

II If everybody was satisfied with himself, there would be no heroes. *II*
Mark Twain

You will remember that we spoke about fear as a projection into the future – a future event appearing real. Although we know fear to be at heart an illusion, this knowledge is not always enough to eliminate our suffering. And fear can be a great teacher as well as a bringer of gifts. We rarely take the opportunity to look deeply into ourselves, to question the ground on which we stand. When fear and sorrow are present, we are more receptive to learning. Our suffering and our vulnerability allow us to perceive the world differently. It's uncomfortable. Hard. The process of rebirth or recreation is often painful.

Fear of failure, rejection, ridicule or abandonment lie deeply rooted within each of us. Our survival as infants depends upon winning the nurture and affection of others with greater power or resources than us. When situations reach a point where we fear we may be rejected by those closest to us, our emotions can reach fever pitch.

I was once in this position having left a relationship. I heard the Call, that it was time to move on. I was young, passionate, attractive, I didn't need to hold on to something that wasn't working. But somehow, I couldn't quite break free. No matter which ways I tried, I found myself drawn back to my ex. I got more and more frustrated and frightened as increasing amounts of energy went into taking my attention off this person. I couldn't sleep. The weight fell off me. My behaviour became erratic, my moods swung wildly. I literally had no idea what I was going to do or say or believe next. Having scared myself witless (and no doubt him too), with my unpredictability, I felt my sanity was holding on by a thread. I had to put in place an intense set of rules and regulations and sit with my battle until the desperation passed. This experience was humbling, horrific, scary and undoubtedly transformative for me. Until I had walked the dark night of the soul I was not in a position to be able to genuinely hold a light for others. Agonizing and confusing as this experience was, I don't regret it as it helped me to become a better coach and a more compassionate human being.

Whatever pains your trials are currently causing you – wherever the inner critic and self doubt want to go today, can you hold on to the possibility that there is a gift of transformation in it for you?

What could your trials be teaching you?

Managing Your Mind

Resilience, our emotional fitness, the ability to endure, is a key quality for surviving the emotional agonies of a Supreme Ordeal. Whether it is grief, loss, defeat or anxiety that we need to meet head on, our ability to feel the pain and continue, determines how and when we emerge out the other side.

Our inner critic, with its bullying and unkind tone, can eliminate confidence, sap our enthusiasm and kill our passion if we let it. We need to arm ourselves with an equally powerful inner cheerleader, to come to our defense when our berating voice is blaring at full volume.

Look at any of our sporting heroes and you will see this agony and ecstasy in action. Andy Murray, restorer of the bruised ego of British tennis, went through a slew of defeats, challenges and battles over the years. He seemed to continually fall at the last hurdle. His tipping point came with the hire of Ivan Lendl as his coach. Aside from helping Andy to make the most of his form, skills and physical ability, Lendl also taught him to work effectively to harness the power and focus of his mind.

How is it that Lendl knew how to help Andy? Because he had been there. He had also managed to lose four Grand Slams in a row during his career in tennis. But he turned it around and had a terrific run of success in the eighties and nineties. Andy needed to know how he did it. The combination of tools they used were:

- Positive self-talk,
- Visualization, and
- Impulse control.

1. Positive Self-Talk

We need to find the ways in which we can be our own best friend. We need to learn to be our defender, a warrior and a coach to stretch and challenge ourselves. Talking kindly to ourselves, in the soft tones we would use for a frightened child or animal, can help immensely at these times. We need to allay the anxiety and address our need for safety before we can think clearly about next steps. We need to work with the part of ourselves that feels defeated and incapable, offering it positive affirmation and stimulus to move through the latest challenge into the calm after the storm.

If you have children or animals of your own or are close to those belonging to others, you will know this voice. The one that greets the grazed knee, the absent teddy bear or the lost and scared. The part of you that is just doing the best he or she can and is now run ragged.

What does the child within you need to hear?

You don't need to offer your comfort out loud, but you do need to find the place in you that needs to hear it.

 Take a moment now. Put your hand in the place where there is wounding or pain or discomfort in your body. Your heart? Your guts? Your throat? Rest a warm hand there and talk kindly and gently to that part of you. It needs your attention.

- What are the cruelest jibes and tricks that your inner critic plays on you?
- What is the counterbalance statement you need to make?

You may also find it helpful to try journaling. Take out a piece of paper or a notebook and just begin a conversation with yourself. See if you can describe and pinpoint how you feel. See if you can uncover where the voice is coming from. If the strength behind your Quest were to say something to that pain, what support would it offer? What would your mentor say?

2. Visualization Tools

Scientists are just starting to discover how we can use the power of our minds to do extraordinary things. Recent research has indicated that focusing our mind's attention on injured parts of our bodies can speed up healing. Sportspeople have long known about the power of visualization.

Taking ten minutes per day to visualize yourself at the end of the Quest can help to bolster your confidence when you are at a low ebb. Imagine yourself at the completion of the Quest, achieving and enjoying the experience of success. Are you holding a healthy child? Signing your first book deal? Seeing your clients succeed in their health/career/life challenges?

You may use this tool to keep you calm and serene in the face of challenge. Alternatively it might work best for you to imagine a positive result, leaving you energized and excited.

A useful format for visualization is the ideal scene. In Chapter 4, I asked you to describe what life would be like if you achieved your Quest. A way through the challenges of the Belly of the Whale is to reorient yourself and your subconscious to these goals. You do this through reading aloud your ideal scene, 100 times over. Take time to feel all the emotions that pass through you as you do this. You do not need to do this all in one go. Five or 10 times a day over a period of weeks will be enough to reinforce your direction and bring you the strength to continue.

3. Impulse Control

When we are battling our inner demons, we can find it very hard to find perspective. The stress we put ourselves under manifests itself in our body. The first place you find this stress is in the breath. When we are anxious our breathing becomes more frequent and shallow, causing our bodies to be deprived of oxygen. If we learn to control our breath, we are better able to control our mind.

The simplest form of mindfulness simply involves closing your eyes and observing your breath. All you need do is watch and name the "in" and the "out" breath. Take time now to try it. Close your eyes. Focus on the bottom of your nose, where air enters through your nostrils and just watch and name.

A 2009 study by the University of North Carolina observed through MRI scans that those who practice regular mindfulness have better cognition, more balanced emotional responses and higher levels of immunity.

So as the Buddhist joke goes, don't just do something, sit there!

Mind Your Inner Language

Our negative nature loves to keep us stuck. The inner critic has a way of hitting home and creating inner pain in a more potent way than most external forces. We can find ourselves crippled by the voice in our head unless we take some action to manage it. One way to do this is to mind our inner language. Usually our internal questioning concerning ourselves and our situation is quite disempowered. Why is this happening to me? Why can't I just get a grip? The answers to these kinds of questions are likely to breed more negativity and despair. When we begin to notice the quality of our questioning, we can change the experience that the questions give us. If we ask a more empowered question, we are likely to engage in a more constructive inner conversation. Empowered questions focus on the possibilities available to us. They include:

- "How can I make this situation more enjoyable?"
- "What is the best next step I can take?"

 "Who do I know who could help me with this?"

Write down three empowered questions that could help you to see things differently during the grand challenge stage of this Quest.

-
-
-

Maintaining Momentum

> **"** The ultimate measure of a man is not
> where he stands in moments of comfort
> and convenience, but where he stands
> at times of challenge and controversy. **"**
> *Martin Luther King Jr.*

When the drudge of putting one foot in front of the other hits, it can be easy to lose your momentum. The wonder and energy that greeted your acceptance of the Quest is over and the fanfare of departure far behind you. It has grown quiet and lonely; you are in the dark belly of your work. At these times, it is important to reach out for support and for company. Spend time with people who make you laugh; find opportunities to learn – whether through free podcasts, books, seminars, great conversations or time with your mentor. All of these can provide sustenance in the lonely time.

- What music makes you feel most inspired and happy?
- What images, thoughts, ideas, bring you joy and inspiration?
- Who do you need to spend time with to recharge your batteries and zest?

Changing your environment or company can also help to move out of this state. I don't want you to run away from the wisdom that sits in uncomfortable feelings. But at the same time, if you know you have isolated yourself from the support you need or it really is time to take a walk, do that. Find a way to reconnect and receive help to move your energy.

Things that I personally have found helpful to move through pain or anxiety include:

1. Natural and movement – going for a walk in nature, dancing or running, listening to music or the radio.

2. Help – giving service to other people, listening to them or helping out somehow.

3. Reaching out – for love, support and encouragement.

Whether you do it on paper internally or speak it out, you do need to articulate where you are right now, however tough that feels. By being in touch with your vulnerability, frailty and sensitivity, you make it possible to move through.

- What do you need to say or have heard to help you shift gear?
- Who can you spend time with to remind yourself of who you are and the progress you have made toward where you are going?

Patience and Persistence

"It will never work. It's hopeless."

So sayeth the inner voice.

And it might be right.

So, can we learn to be OK with the fact that it may not work? Nothing in life comes with a "satisfaction guaranteed" sticker. You might put in a phenomenal amount of effort toward your Quest and yet may not get the outcome you were so hoping for in the time you have invested in it. The key Question is, are you willing to put forward that effort nonetheless?

Atticus Finch is a small-town lawyer fighting for justice in the book, *To Kill a Mockingbird*. He teaches his children the importance of justice, courage and standing up for what's right: "Courage is not a man with a gun in his hand. It's knowing you're licked before you begin but you begin anyway and see it through no matter what. You rarely win, but sometimes you do."

Our internal drives are impatient. We want to have everything now, just the way we think it should be. We forget that there is a process in which things happen and that there is no way round but to honour that process however slow, painful or circuitous it might be. Einstein worked for years as a patent office clerk to fund himself while he worked on his theories. Cezanne produced his best work in his sixties and it took him a long and winding road to get there. Our mindset may need to be "it takes as long as it takes." Like the female mountaineers in Chapter 9, we may discover that a whole other Quest needs to happen before we continue on our path. Or that our aspirations do not match our practical reality.

We need to learn to cultivate patience. To see the Hero's Journey as a spiral rather than a straight line. We may not get exactly what we had hoped for first time round. But the experience of the journey better equips us to try again. If there is anything to be learned from our Questing ancestors, it is that perseverance eventually pays off. The Greek philosopher Heraclitus told us "You never step in the same river twice." If you need to go back and try again, you are different and have grown and the situation is never a carbon copy of your previous encounter.

The Stories We Tell Ourselves

The reason that fears and doubts are a risk to us is not because of the future possibility we see in them. Instead it is about the leap we take that goes: "If this doesn't work out it will mean that I am _____."

It is not what happens or might happen, it is what we will make it mean about ourselves that is crippling.

Shakespeare's play, *Hamlet*, concerns a troubled hero who is asked by the ghost of his father to avenge his murder. Hamlet takes all manner of unnecessary actions because he is distracted and consumed by his own obsessive thinking. Our thoughts can overwhelm and distress us.

Looking at our fears and doubts on paper can help us to navigate a way through them. But first we have to name them. This exercise is a useful one if you are becoming paralyzed by fear or doubt.

Complete the sentences. . . .

- I am afraid that . . .
- I think that it is unlikely that I will . . .
- What am I making this mean about who I am and what I can do?

Each of these statements shows us a world of horrors that exists only within our head. Our battles with these inner demons can be won only by seeing them for what they are. Illusions. Tricks of the light.

Take your list of "what this means about me." Revise each statement so it begins: I release the idea that . . .

For example, if I believe that if I don't win this art competition, it will mean that there is no future for me as an artist, I could say:

"I release the idea that there is no future for me as an artist."

You are then going to replace this belief with a more positive one that reflects the truth of your situation. Not an overstatement that you do not believe, but an alternative possibility for yourself.

"The truth is, I am learning more about my practice with every brush stroke."

Have a go right now.

A Lifetime's Preparation

Often our worry and fear proves misplaced. We are better prepared, more resourceful and readier than we thought. We can surprise ourselves.

The poet, David Whyte's big break came at a conference when a key speaker cancelled. He describes trying to prepare for days beforehand and somehow not being able to focus or concentrate. When he arrived at the podium, in front of 3000 watchful faces, he had nothing scripted, but he realized as he looked at them and they looked at him, "that his whole life had been a preparation for that moment."

In what ways have you "prepared your whole life" for this Quest?

A History of Graft

You will never have read Wendy Cope's first poem, or listened to Eric Clapton's first song or eaten Jamie Oliver's first soufflé. Why? Because what we see of successful people in the world is the end point of a huge amount of work they have put in.

When we release our expectations of how something will be, we are free to enjoy whatever turns up. No doubt we will have dreamed about this moment, putting our own gloss and story into the future picture. We humans tend to see in black and white. In polarities. Everything will be perfect. Everyone will be wonderful. The earth will move. Or, it'll be a disaster. It's going to be a nightmare. I will be humiliated.

If you find yourself at either end of the spectrum, you might find it useful to explore what else could be true. Life will be what it is. If you have done all you can to prepare for this moment, the rest is in the lap of the gods.

" Heroes are made by the paths they choose, not the powers they are graced with. *"*
Brodi Ashton, Everneath

Above all, keep taking action. Keep experimenting. Take one small step and then another. Keep tabs on the bird's eye view and the worm's eye view. Glance up to the summit and find the heart to take the next step. And then another. Have faith. You have made preparations, you have chosen your new future. You are going to keep on keeping on until you get there.

I believe in you. Do you?

 ## Chapter Summary

- Our most frightening battles are the ones that take place internally.

- Everyone imposes limits on themselves and has to work consciously to free themselves from them.

- On the Quest, persistence, patience and perseverance always pay off.

- We will always reach a result although it may not be what we expected or may not give us what we thought it would.

- Learning to self-manage is critical – using healthy habits and mindset tools to help us become more resilient and get more done.

- We need to take care of ourselves and acknowledge our vulnerability – a Quest would not be a Quest if it weren't a real and genuine challenge.

YOUR QUEST

- Remind yourself of your Quest here.

- Remind yourself of how you will know you have achieved it.

- Remind yourself of what you stand for.

- Remind yourself of the qualities you have to support you.

- What progress have you have made?

- What have you learned?

- What gratitudes do you want to share:

    - With yourself

    - With others

    - With the journey of the Quest itself?

Part Four

THE RETURN

In which we recover from our trials, discover what
we have learned and get out the paper hats.

11

COMING HOME

II The greatness of a man is not in
how much wealth he acquires
but in his integrity and his ability
to affect those around him positively. *II*
Bob Marley

When he wasn't making music, Bob Marley was catalyzing social change. In the film *Marley*, there's a very powerful piece of footage of Bob. He is outside his home, receiving and welcoming locals and handing out money. Listening to their troubles and their aims, he gives each person who visits enough financial support to help them make a difference in their own lives.

What a hero.

To give back, like Bob, to share the wisdom and experience you gained in the Quest, is the final part of the Hero's Journey. In the great heroes' stories, the main character often returns from their Quest with a "boon" or token of some kind. It could be a message, a symbol or a new way of seeing the world. This gift is a by-product of their journey.

Not every Hero's Journey ends in triumph. Questing can be exhausting, both emotionally and physically. We may not receive the result we were most hoping for. Or the end of the Quest might leave a hole in our lives that we are uncomfortable with, but do not yet know how to fill.

The Return is the space in between. It is the long out-breath. The drawn-out sigh. It is the silent dawn over the battlefield the day after the war. The Return brings us down to earth with a thud. It is time to stop, slow down and listen. No more of the urgency and speed that characterizes a Quest. Instead, this is a period of drawing in on ourselves, consolidating what we have learned and preparing to share it with the wider world.

The Return requires us to re-cross the threshold between the extraordinary and the ordinary. Returning from the intense colours of the Questing space, into the more muted sounds and smells of the day-to-day. This can prove a difficult transition. We have seen so much, done so much that most people cannot understand.

We feel transformed by our experience. We may struggle to reintegrate.

This chapter then, is about the making of this transition. We need to take time to consolidate, to recognize the journey we have been on and to integrate the lessons we have learned. We need to find ways to transition back into the day-to-day reality, integrate our experience and find ways to share the gifts of this experience with others. Much like the start of the Quest, we need to ask ourselves "What will I take with me and what will I leave behind?"

Quiet Time

II After the ecstasy, the laundry . . . *II*
Jack Kornfield

In the immediate time after our Quest is completed, we may simply need to rest and relax. Taking time to recuperate and recover, where possible, is very important. On a physical level, we may have exerted ourselves beyond our limits. The extraordinary energy of the Quest may have let your body do more than you knew it possibly could. You are likely to feel it afterwards. Emotionally, you may also be in need of restoration. Perhaps you had to put aside your feelings in order to do what had to be done. Or perhaps the range of emotions you felt were startling, frightening or exhilarating. Allowing your emotional body the chance to calm down is crucial if you are to integrate your experience.

- What action do you need to take to recover from your Quest?
- How can you take care of yourself after your Quest?

In the quiet time, we may find ourselves processing the journey we have taken. We may be saying farewell to those who have travelled with us. We may be frightened about reintegrating into the world of those who have not seen and shared the experiences we have been through.

Many members of the military and armed forces really struggle to return to "civilian" life. The rules, language, social norms and hierarchies that govern combat are very different to those found in regular life. Veterans often struggle to explain how their skills transfer into the world of civilian work. In fact, this has been such a problematic issue, that the Obama administration recently introduced a "reverse boot camp" to help former soldiers adjust to the post-military environment and translate their experience in ways that prospective employers can understand.

Your transition may not feel as extreme as those of the veterans, but for many of you, life will have changed significantly. You may need time to find the voice to describe your experiences and your journey. For others of you it will be a struggle to stop talking about them!

What You Take With, What You Leave Behind

Some new mothers describe grieving the physical emptiness that comes from the translocation of their little one from a companion inside them, to a unique and distinct individual out in the world. They can experience the post-natal period as a rush of painful, confusing and unfamiliar feelings accompanying the struggle to adjust. New mums can also report feeling sorrow and grief for the loss of the freedom and independence that they had before mother-hood and guilt that these feelings exist.

Theatre actors often describe the phenomenon of "post-show depression." A vacuum opens up where rehearsals, camaraderie and focus on the role used to be. We may have been part of a very tight team, working together to achieve an objective; the film being in the can, the operation completed, the last exam taken. This means that the team needs to disband. For students graduating from university or college, this might be the first time that they experience their peers taking separate and divergent paths, with everyone needing to find their own way in the world. These experiences can be disorientating and take a while to adjust to.

Having lived life at a high-adrenalin, high-octane pace as we Quested, we may feel unsure about how we will live without this driving force operating in our lives. Post 2012 Olympics, some of the worlds' top athletes have spoken openly of their struggle to identify their next steps. Having worked tremendously hard to earn their opportunity to perform and having been steeped in glory and had the attention of the world on them, they suddenly find them-selves in need of a source of income and operating as ordinary people. Those who do not have stable families and work to return to can feel the rug has been pulled out from underneath their feet. Some of the jobs our international Olympians do alongside their sport include: acting, teaching, fire fighting, farming, writing, plumbing and the law.

The Afterward

American, Ruby Wax, started her working life as a comedian, but having gained a Master's degree in Mindfulness-based Cognitive Behavioural Therapy from Oxford University, she now runs seminars as a leadership communication specialist. In a recent article, she described the enormity of the career change Quest she was on. Once she had finally made it through to secure her place, it was a real rite of passage to spend time studying in some of Oxford's most iconic buildings. "I almost passed out with joy the first time I went to the Bodleian Library," she says.

Rituals and rites of passage can offer us a way to process and mark our entry into a new stage of life or re-integration into the "ordinary" world. These can take the form of a ceremony, a party or a graduation. Participants in the Quest need the space to share stories, and say their thank yous and farewells. People often enjoy receiving and sharing tokens that evidence their experience – photographs, memorabilia, class of 2013 clothing etc. On returning from the war, my Russian grandfather began planting trees in memory of his fallen friends. Our desire to memorialize is part of what makes us human and helps ease transition and integration.

To mark the achievements of a Quest, you might like to create your own graduation. Instead of a formal ceremony that takes place at the end of an education experience, construct a way of celebrating your own right of passage. In Subud, a spiritual practice first established in Indonesia, the evolution of our soul's development or the acquisition of additional skills is sometimes marked by changing your name. This might be a bit much for most of us, but it offers a way of recognizing development and change. Have you moved from qualified osteopath to experienced osteopath? Have you gone from maiden to mother? Mark it. Have you moved from a life of addiction to recovery? What name or title best describes your new way of being? Have you completed a project you thought was over-ambitious? How can you describe the skills your experience has given you?

If you were to claim your Quest experience in the form of a name what would it be and why?

Humans also build associations between our physical body and the journeys we have taken. I still have a fabulous scar on my calf from the exhaust pipe of a Thai motorbike that I got when I was there in 1998. Tattoos are our way of marking events on our body. In traditional cultures across Africa, including Benin, Nigeria and Tanzania, native custom includes the rite of scarification, where deliberate scars and marks are made on the body to signify the transition into adulthood. Our "battle scars" of birth or recovery can act as reminders of where our Quest has taken us.

Consider your own journey.

- Are there events you need to mark in order to "close" this chapter of your life?
- Who needs to be involved? What simple ritual might you put in place to mark the Quest?

Adjusting as We Cross the Threshold

Sometimes we may even struggle with whether to return at all. We may be unsure about whether we will be welcome. We may be anxious about how others will see us now, or whether the environment will be hospitable for who we now are. When the Greek hero Odysseus returns home after 10 years of war, he disguises himself first as a beggar. He is keen to find out how things stand in his kingdom and to test his wife's loyalty before he is willing to reveal himself.

We can feel this way too. Knowing that our experiences have changed us, it is natural to feel uncertain about how others' perception of us may have changed. Musician and ex-BT employee, Max

Fraser talks about the aftermath of being in an internationally recognized band:

> "I am still negotiating the impact of the experience of being in Faithless. After 16 years of doing it I still feel like a wide-eyed schoolboy. It is staggering to me. No part of me feels famous. People stop you in the street. When people see someone they recognize, they scowl at you. I grew up as a black boy in England in the sixties. They scowled at you then. Not in a good way. So when people look at me weird when I pop to the shops I have to remind myself "Oh yeah, I was on Top of The Pops last night."

When we have been on the adventure of a lifetime, the idea of re-entering the world may simply feel too much to bear. In which case, you may find yourself struggling to return at all.

The 1968 *Sunday Times* Golden Globe race was the first non-stop, single-handed, round-the-world yacht race. It was organized around the ideas of French sailor and author, Bernard Moitessier, who was planning to circumnavigate the globe that year. Bernard was unimpressed with the materialism of the race, feeling that it compromised the spirit of his intention to pit himself against the elements for the sake of the challenge itself, not for the winnings. And so, instead of stopping once he had completed one circumnavigation, he abandoned the race altogether whilst in a strong position to win and carried on for another half-round of the globe, finally landing in Tahiti in 1969.

Who Am I Now?

In The Return, we begin to uncover the practicalities of who we are now. We are transformed, irrevocably, by the experience we have created. We have gone from single woman to mother. From addicted to clean living. From UK citizen to Englishman in New York. We may need to re-learn our approach to life because it looks and feels quite different. Blinking into the daylight after our time underground, we can learn to be patient, gentle and kind with ourselves. We are reborn. We may need a little to stand independently on our new feet. We may find we need a little ballast to help us to ground ourselves after the adventure. This is where family, friends and routines we may have neglected whilst on the Quest and a return to the simple things in life, can prove very valuable.

- What are the elements of your return that need attention?
- What structures, people and habits do you have to fall back on?
- How could you ground yourself?

What If You Didn't Get There?

> ❞ A goal is not always meant to be reached.
> Sometimes it serves as something to aim at. ❞
> *Bruce Lee*

Maybe you feel that you did not reach the goal you set yourself when you began your Quest. I wonder then if you are looking at the external symbols of success or the internal state of being that you wanted to create. Consider the experience you were looking for. How close did you come to having that?

> ❞ Whatever happens, whether the film gets
> picked up for distribution or not, I know
> that we have all done something exceptional
> and learned a huge amount from it. And
> now we have each other as a network too. ❞
> *Sica Denerly-Weiss, on the upcoming film* One,
> *www.one-themovie.co.uk*

If your Quest did not give you that moment of expansion, happiness, challenge, security or adventure that you were looking for, that just means that the way remains open for you to discover it.

It may be that you are already standing on buried treasure. In *The Alchemist*, Paulo Coelho's modern fable, the main character Santiago, travels all over the world only to discover that the treasure he has been pursuing lay buried in his own back garden.

Perhaps your Quest is actually an inward rather than an outward journey and the joys of it wait patiently for you to discover them?

> *II* A hobnail casket of jewels found in a tree
> hollow should be fondled before it is opened.
> Its lock may have rusted or broken away from
> the clasp. Still you should touch the nail heads,
> and test its weight. No smashing with an ax
> head before it is decently exhumed from the
> grave that has hidden it all this time. No gasp
> at a miracle that is truly miraculous because
> the magic lies in the fact that you knew
> it was there for you all along. *II*
> *Toni Morrison,* Beloved

It is also possible that your Quest is not finished. Quests can undergo a hiatus or delay. But they need not be abandoned forever. Perhaps a change in circumstances forces a pause or a redirection. Perhaps you have experienced too many rejections in a row and need to take a break before you throw yourself back into the fray. Don't give up for good. Just take a breather. Accomplishing something that really matters to you could well be a lifetime's work – and what an interesting and rewarding lifetime that could be. Camila Batmanghelidjh, founder of Kids Company, a charity that transforms the lives of thousands of neglected and abused children in the UK, struggled for many years to even get funding for her vision. Now the cuts have bitten again, but she remains determined in her vocation. She says, "It really is about bringing about a systemic transformation in the way we care for young people.

I want to see political change and I haven't finished the job. And maybe I won't. All I can tell you is that the day I am on my death-bed, I will be genuinely happy with the way my life panned out."

Oliver Burkeman of *The Guardian* emphasizes the importance of seeing progress with every solution you invest energy in.

II For complex problems, trying one solution and getting upset when it fails is preposterous: any single solution is likely to fail. The mindset we need isn't the positive-thinking mantra that failure is impossible; it's that failures are inevitable, and for good reason. *II*
From "This Column Will Change Your Life",
The Guardian, 6 November 2010

Persistence and perseverance will almost always pay off as long as you remain creative about how to get there. If you are on the wrong path, listen carefully to your body, intuition and the feedback from your world and you will eventually find the right course. Malcolm Gladwell, bestselling author, was rejected by 18 ad agencies before he became a writer by default. Sailor Ellen MacArthur might have become a vet were it not for being really ill in her final year at school.

Could there be some sort of gift in the adversity you have experienced?

Is there a Course Correction that your Quest is trying to offer you?

Lessons Learned

Whether your Quest exceeded or fell far short of your expectations, there is plenty for us to learn when we reflect back on the journey we have been on. Questing is an iterative process – as long as the price has not been too high, we are likely to want to try again – perhaps on a larger scale, or in a different form. When we reflect back we can see with hindsight the twists, turns and choice points. We can take time to evaluate what worked well for us and what we would like to have done differently or avoided. This is the way that your wisdom is built, incrementally, with new knowledge acquired through experience and practice.

Before, during or after the fanfare of The Return, at a point not too distant from now, take some time out, individually and with your team, to reflect in a structured way about your process. You will be amazed what you discover when you have the time to think things through.

Lisa-Marie Taylor is the volunteer coordinator of the Radical Feminism conference in London. Over a cup of tea, we had the chance to look at all the different elements of the Quest to bring 1000 women under one roof and provide an agenda that would be relevant to their diverse needs and interests. Along the way to the event, Lisa-Marie began identifying opportunities to do things better – purely through trial and error. After the event, she will be able to consolidate this experience alongside that of her colleagues. This will make life easier for the next time round, helping them to capitalize on what works and reduce friction and challenges along the way. The first Quest is always a bumpy ride.

One of my clients, Jordana, runs a wonderful millinery business called Fancier Feather (www.fancierfeather.co.uk).

We recently worked together on a lessons learned review of her bespoke millinery service. Her client was demanding, the process and interaction left Jordana feeling cheated and disappointed. By working through this process we were able to identify actions she could take to change the experience and help everyone feel clear. These included – terms and conditions, taking deposits, when and how to send designs, a transparent process and costing model. It also included a fair price for a unique product.

Questions to ask yourself during a lessons learned review:

- What worked well?
- How effectively did we manage our/my/the clients' expectations and relationships?
- What do we never want to happen again?
- Knowing what we know now, what would we like to do differently?
- What opportunities did we have that we would like to capitalize on next time?
- What do I need to put in place to help the process run more smoothly next time?

And Now What?

" Dreaming about being an actress, is more exciting than being one. "
Marilyn Monroe

You may have got to the end of your Quest and not be sure that the result was worth the effort. Have no fear. With your lessons learned and your experience, you are still in a strong position to share your experience with others. No Quest is ever wasted. The full purpose of your Quest may yet be revealed.

Once you have got to the top of your game and had the experience you most wanted, then what do you do? You could keep repeating your Quest on a larger and larger scale. You could broaden your Quest out into other areas. You could tell others how to do what you did. You could retire and make merry. Or you could do something completely different.

Ellen MacArthur held the record for sailing single-handedly around the world. Box ticked! She describes pondering what her next move would be, "I became interested in how finite resources are, from being on a boat. Knowing that you only have a certain amount of food, water and fuel. I wanted to explore how we as a civilization could transfer to a more circular and sustainable economy." To this end, she set up her foundation, which offers educational opportunities and grants related to innovation.

We need to make sure that we are able to integrate the experience we have been through to avoid falling back into old patterns. Those leaving prison or rehabilitation share that it is once we are out of treatment or a contained space that the real work begins. Can we find a way in the world, to use and apply what we have learned for the good of others?

 What could your Quest teach you about how to live?

Celebration and Gratitude

So now, finally, we are ready to celebrate. We have found our way back home, taken time to recover and have taken what we can out of the experience. If you are an Alpha type of hero, you may already be planning your next adventure before you have closed the door and taken your shoes off. Or perhaps you are someone who struggles to acknowledge your achievements, because you have a story about not being enough. Learning to recognize your progress and reward yourself is important. Remember your inner five-year-old? The motor for your motivation? You may think it is silly or embarrassing or whatever to celebrate your success – but they don't! Your inner five-year-old is looking for streamers, party poppers, cake and lots of prizes. Your reward needs to be meaningful to you.

Find a way to really recognize all that you have accomplished. It takes huge courage to step outside the crowd and choose to align with what really matters to you. Questing will only ever constitute a real success if you are able to recognize your own achievement.

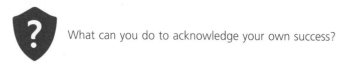 What can you do to acknowledge your own success?

II It is better to light a single candle
than to curse the darkness. *II*
W.L. Watkinson

So now it is time to take your big heart, your hard-earned smarts and your personal strength out into the world and help others to shine. In these uncertain times, the world has never been in more need of real life, everyday heroes.

12

BEING THE HERO IN EVERYDAY LIFE

" The fishermen know that the sea is
dangerous and the storm terrible, but
they have never found these dangers
sufficient reason for remaining ashore. *"*
Vincent van Gogh

Why Your Story Matters

" A story is like water
that you heat for your bath.
It takes messages between the fire
and your skin. It lets them meet,
and it cleans you! *"*
Jalaluddin Rumi, Story Water

I first learned about the Hero's Journey whilst training as a story-teller. I got to spend five weeks with people from all over the world, hearing their stories of struggle and change and hope. Stories of childhood, adolescence, their first jobs, their first children. Stories about ageing and wisdom. Stories of adventure and of loss. This experience was transformative for me. I realized how much my soul was fed by the stories of others. These were even better than the imaginary ones I found in books. These stories can teach you more about the world and about how to live in it.

Once upon a Quest . . .

There are so many ways for you to tell the story of your Quest. And so many people who would benefit from hearing it. Whether you are just beginning to envision what your Quest might be, whether you are in the early stages, the Belly of the Whale or out the other side. Just by the fact that you are now aware of the Quest as an option for living your life means you are ready to tell your tales.

Stories speak to us. Irrespective of generations, backgrounds and gender, they speak to the universality of our experience. Everyone you meet has been with joy and sorrow. Everyone will know love and everyone will know loss. Every being on this earth values its life and existence. As I write this, my little cat, Fat Brian, is snuggled up beside me. His beingness matters to him. His story matters!

You can start small. Tell your pet. Speak your story into the air. Try it on for size. Then tell another living person what you know. Then play it bigger. Do a talk. Make a video. Write a report. An article. A blog. Make a feature film or documentary. Start a campaign. Preach it.

Tell the truth. Share your purpose, your intention, your vows. Your trials and tribulations. We are most connected when we hear someone speak from the heart. Don't worry about tripping up or missing out on a detail. It is your story, so you cannot possibly get it wrong.

Think about your motive and your audience. Do you want to share inspiration? Or to teach a new skill or perspective? What is the best way to tell the story to the people you are with? What will matter the most to them?

Life itself is one magical Hero's Journey. On your return to the earth and air from which you came, what legacy do you want to offer to those who come after? What change or contribution do you wish to have made? What do you want people to say about how you served after you have gone?

 What is the story that only you can tell?

Questing for Life

II Reach high, for the stars lie hidden in you. Dream deep, for every dream precedes the goal. *II*
Rabindranath Tagore

Joseph Campbell talked often about the importance of "finding your bliss." Given the choice between the practical, logical and sensible, and the path of adventure, he wished to give us all permission to embrace the latter. Toni Morrison, Nobel Prize-winning writer and one of my personal heroes, commented in a recent interview that life could be lived on the flat line and the rollercoaster. If I have done a good enough job here I do hope that I have persuaded you to choose the rollercoaster.

Alongside the grandeur of what is now possible for you, with your inner hero activated and alive inside you, there is also the "ordinary" world. How does your new sense of being the hero in your own story impact on how you treat yourself and others? How does it impact on what you accept or challenge? On how you speak, act, dress, behave and think? Your actions will drown out any of your words. What can you do to line up what you say you believe in and stand for, with how you act – at the bus stop, in the kitchen or online?

Start small and improve your life daily. See if you can find a way to be a light to others in the small things. These are just as important as the big ones. See what needs solving and take action to solve it. Not everything has to be a grand gesture. Small is beautiful. Quest a life well lived. Embrace the happiness that a sense of purpose will give you.

 Consider collecting the stories of others. When an older person dies it is as though a whole library goes up in flames. We need to hold on to these stories of where we have come from. Use your Questing skills to create a narrative from the history and lives of those in your community whose story goes unheard.

In the time after our transformative Quest, we are afforded an opportunity to bring the light and wisdom of experience to others. The Winston Churchill Trust (www.wcmt.org.uk) considers the sharing of knowledge acquired on a transforming journey to be a key "output" of the journey itself:

> "We have been enabling people to travel overseas for almost 50 years, and we never cease to be amazed at the transformation that such an experience can bring about in an individual. Fellows frequently tell us that their confidence, independence and motivation have grown immeasurably as a result of the experiences and challenges of their Fellowship journeys. They have returned to their occupations in the UK with renewed enthusiasm and inspiration, and have been able to make a real difference to other people in terms of new ideas, best practice and leadership."

And They All Lived Happily Ever After

There's a board game called Othello that purports to take "a minute to learn and a lifetime to master." Many of the skills of the Quest are like this. We can intellectually understand how mistakes are a crucial part of learning, but can we forgive ourselves as the stakes get higher, the risks of failure more likely or the impact of an error more painful? Of course, I wish for you to aim high. I believe you can use your Life Planning skills to play an ever-larger game. You now have a solid foundation from which to grow and it is your choice in which direction you decide to build and what you choose to create.

Your uniqueness determines the right Quest for you. Whatever the next Call that draws you, you can trust that you have the qualities and capabilities to achieve it. Fiona Harrold describes this in *Be Your Own Life Coach*:

> "I have discovered, without exception, that the dream that each person has is totally in keeping with who they are and, as a result, totally achievable."

Perform the service of being unreasonable, when and where it is justified. Claiming your life and your right to live it as fully and powerfully as you can is a form of activism. Stretching for something new or better is an inspiration and beacon to others. You owe it to those who do not have the choices and freedoms that you do. "Your acting small does not serve the world," writes Marianne Williamson, spiritual teacher, author and lecturer.

See every experience as an opportunity to learn and grow.

What Is Your Way of Walking in This World?

As you head off into the sunset and our time together draws to an end, I wish to offer you a parting gift. A memento of our time together. An English teacher shared this last poem with me when I was a young girl. It's been a great anchor for me ever since and I offer it to you and encourage you to live a heroic expanded life throughout all your todays and tomorrows.

Go. Stand for something. Stretch beyond the ordinary. Be bold, be true to yourself, be the hero of your own life.

Success

To live well, to laugh often, to love much,
to gain the respect of intelligent people,
to win the love of little children.

To fill one's niche and accomplish one's task,
to leave the world better than one finds it,
whether by a garden patch,
a perfect poem
or another life ennobled.

To never lack appreciation of earth's beauty or fail to express it,
to always look for the best in others,
to give the best one has.

To make one's life an inspiration
and one's memory a benediction.

This is success.

Bessie Anderson Stanley, based on the poem, *Success*, 1904

FURTHER READING AND REFERENCES

If you enjoyed this book, the adventure continues online. Visit www.yourlifeplan.com for free tools, resources and the opportunity to participate in e-courses that explore the material in more depth. If you fancy following me on Twitter, its either @lifeplanbook or @thelifeproject. Ditto for Facebook.

To apply to the Winston Churchill Trust for a once in a lifetime international travel research bursary, please visit: www.wcmt.org.uk

For more information on multiple intelligences and to take the test visit: www.literacyworks.org/mi/assessment/findyourstrengths.html

To take the hero typology test devised by Carole Pearson visit: www.capt.org/pmai-assessment

I also highly recommend the work of Insight Seminars – they offer great training in Questing for Life all over the world, in the form of their weekend seminar programmes. You can visit their website at www.insightseminars.org

Poetry

Come to the Edge, *New Numbers*, Christopher Logue, 1969
Tilicho Lake, *Where Many Rivers Meet*, David Whyte, Many Rivers Press, 1990
Success, Bessie Anderson Stanley, 1904

Books

Sacred Contracts: Awakening your Divine Potential, Caroline Myss, Bantam, 2002

Thank God it's Monday, Charles Cameron and Suzanne Elusorr, Ebury Press, 1986

The Hero with a Thousand Faces, Joseph Campbell, Fontana Press, 1993

The Thirst for Wholeness, Christina Grof, HarperSanFrancisco, 1994

The Souls Code, James Hillman, Bantam, 1997

Care of the Soul, Thomas Moore, Piatkus, 2012

Why Me, Why This, Why Now?, Robin Norwood, Tarcher, 2013

Whack on the Side of the Head, Roger von Oech, Business Plus, 2008

The Hero Within, Carole Pearson, HarperSanFrancisco, 1998

A Course in Miracles, Helen Schucman and William T. Thetford, Course in Miracles Society, 2008

ACKNOWLEDGEMENTS

We all stand on the shoulders of giants and so my first thanks need to go to all the excellent thinkers, speakers and adventurers who provide inspiration and evidence to my readers that we can all lead a heroic life.

I'd like to thank all my wonderful family, friends and clients who have acted as sounding boards and champions for this book. Thanks to Jenny and Jonathan at Wiley, for their passion and rigour. Special thanks go to my key readers – Beth T. and Louisa M., for their feedback and encouragement. Thanks also to Francis Briers, Roi Gal-Or and Max Fraser for their inspiration and input. And a big thank you to my darling Peter, without whom this heroine might not have survived the Supreme Ordeal.

ABOUT THE AUTHOR

Image supplied with permission of White Tulip Photography

Erica Sosna is a writer, consultant and speaker whose specialist area is life direction and personal change. Erica uses her expertise as a coach and storyteller to turn complicated concepts into exciting and inspiring talks and tools. Erica offers workshops and one-to-one coaching for individuals to help them discover their Calling and begin their Quest. Erica is also part of the Blessing-White consulting team, offering employee engagement and leadership programmes to world-class businesses across the globe.

For more information about Erica, or to have her speak at your event please visit: www.thelifeproject.co.uk